The Lighted Windows

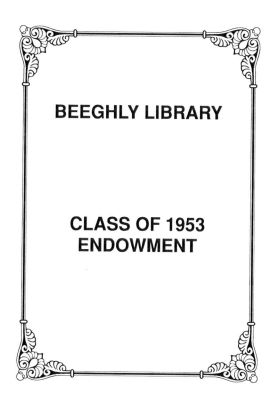

BEEGHLY LIBRARY

**CLASS OF 1953
ENDOWMENT**

Studies in Austrian Literature, Culture, and Thought

Translation Series

Heimito von Doderer

The Lighted Windows
or
The Humanization of the
Bureaucrat Julius Zihal

Translated and with a Foreword
by
John S. Barrett

ARIADNE PRESS
Riverside, California

Ariadne Press would like to express its appreciation to the Austrian Cultural Institute, New York for assistance in publishing this book.

Translated from the German *Die erleuchteten Fenster*
©C.H. Beck'sche Verlagsbuchhandlung, München 1995

Library of Congress Cataloging-in-Publication Data

Doderer, Heimito von, 1896-1966.
    [Erleuchteten Fenster. English]
    The lighted windows, or, The Humanization of the
bureaucrat Julius Zihal / Heimito von Doderer ; translated
and with an afterword by John S. Barrett.
        p.   cm. -- (Studies in Austrian literature, culture,
and thought. Translation series)
    ISBN 1-57241-081-7
    I. Barrett, John S. (John Smith), 1935-   . II. Title.
III. Title: Lighted windows. IV. Title: Humanization of the
bureaucrat Julius Zihal. V. Series.
  PT2607.03E713   2000
  833'.912--dc21
                         99-36365
                           CIP

Cover:
Art: Hannah Barrett
Design: Nancy Jo Haselbacher

Dedicated with the greatest respect
to the
Imperial and Royal Central Tax Assessment Office

by
the Author

FOREWORD

Captured by the Russians on the eastern front in 1916, four years in prisoner of war camps in Siberia, return to a shrunken Austrian homeland in 1920 determined to make a career of writing, following a university education. Newspaper work, bread-and-butter articles, then, finally, modest success as a novelist. Career interrupted by another world war, military service in Russia and France. A prisoner again — this time of the English and only transiently — then another return to Vienna and the hunger years. Not the sort of biography one might expect to give rise to *The Lighted Windows*, a comic tale about a turn-of-the-century Viennese civil servant, written in 1938 at the beginning of the worst of times and published in 1951, as Austria was finally emerging from those times. And it is certainly not the sort of book those times might be expected to bring forth when one recalls that Orwell's *Nineteen Eighty Four* was published just two years before and Salinger's *Catcher in the Rye* in the very same year, and, furthermore, when it turns out that Doderer's novel is written in a style suggesting that its author has never heard of *Ulysses*, Hemingway, Brecht, has never read the starkly worded novels of the German "Group '47" and, in fact, is totally unaware that any novels have been written at all since those of, say, Henry James.

In short, soon after the unusual opening paragraphs have made it clear that this is no ordinary book, the contemporary reader is confronted by two questions: why in the world would anyone take such a roundabout way to tell the rather simple story of a retired bureaucrat who spends his nights watching women in other apartments undress; and why would he tell the story in language that seems to be fussy, old-fashioned, redundant, and laden with similes and metaphors which themselves contribute to the frequent slides from satire into farce?

As the beginning of an answer to the first question, it is worth pointing out that the Vienna into which Heimito von Doderer was born in 1896 was in the throes of modernity — and not just in the fields of art and literature. The great architect Otto Wagner, who shaped the face of Vienna more than anyone else at that time, had just proclaimed that "only the useful can be beautiful" and the high priest of modernity, Adolf Loos, was already creating his totally unadorned, "eyebrowless" buildings and writing about the relationship between ornament and crime. Perhaps even more to the point, Doderer's own father, a civil engineer, was rewarded with a title of nobility for his construction of the new water lines and commuter railways into Vienna — all creations of cast iron, steel, glass, and the straight line. Now, whether it represents the inevitable swing of the generational pendulum or whether — without too strenuous a genuflection toward Dr. Freud — it is related to the author's purportedly often stormy relationship to his father, or whether one chooses to believe the author's statements that such social and personal contexts are totally irrelevant, the fact is that Heimito von Doderer turned away, early in his career, from the prevailing direction of art and culture, away from the practical, away from the straight line. To focus on some small but revealing points: the railroad lines and trains around which Doderer grew up are frequently mentioned in his novels, often as the agents of fate, but the railroad metaphors in the present novel are negative ones: Julius Zihal, our hero, is described as unheedingly and unknowingly passing by the major events in his life like a train clicking though switches as it changes tracks; it is as if the author is saying that direct, apparently purposeful forward motion deprives one of the realization of what is actually taking place within oneself and outside. Or one might consider the difference in outcomes when Julius chooses the direct, point-to-point approach to a certain lady, exemplified by his telescope's straight line of sight, compared to the more circuitous, personal relationship and the eventual walk along the brook in her company after the outing to the vineyards.

In his much longer novel *The Strudelhof Staircase*, published very shortly after *The Lighted Windows*, Doderer puts it more poetically and clearly in the following reference to that famous staircase which permits only a slow, serpentine, contemplative, downward progression from one Vienna neighborhood to another: "The Master of the Staircase has removed a tiny piece from our myriad pathways into the metropolis and showed us how much dignity and decorum is contained in every meter. And because the ramps stretch out flat, or at angles, and run crossways over the incline, preventing purposeful shortcuts and all that climbing around on chicken ladders, our footsteps become words there upon those stages which rise above each other, and if a human being bereft of dignity now appears to be simply forced to carry out his descent more expansively, no matter how come-down he may be, then the deepest intent of the Master of the Staircase is fulfilled, namely, to separate out and display for his fellow citizens and their progeny the splendor of all the small pieces of their pathways through all of their days . . ."

In other words, the author wants us to be *flaneurs*. Like Julius Zihal rambling through parts of his city previously unseen or unnoticed by him, we are asked to take leisurely, even purposeless, strolls with and through Doderer's words as their own leisurely, circuitous cadence — clearly evident in the above example — provides the figurative, verbal equivalent of the reader's mental journey through the landscape being described. In this particular case, the words themselves mimic one's stately progression down the switchback ramps and marble steps. The point is that unless we stroll, even loiter, we will not "see" because we will be "looking for" things with some purpose in mind and that blocks out receptivity. And yet it is precisely the random, unexpected image, like that of Zihal's shoe polish advertisement, which may resonate with dormant memories, unleashing the emotions and reactions that help us to break out of the codified, compressed, sterile modern urban existence. It is, as the narrator says of Julius, ". . . a way out that led through sensations into which one stumbles by chance . . ." It is the beam of sunlight that settles in just the right place, the unsettling, flute-like voices that come from somewhere else, the troubling caress of a floating spider web or a fall breeze. Hence the barrage of similes and metaphors in this novel, very often visual. Each is, in some sense, like Julius' first accidental look out of the window at night, the beginning of a "way out" as well as a level of description different from the direct and purposeful. As the narrator eventually gets around to telling us, it is the "dim and mute process" of humanization, in other words, the "how" rather than the "what," to which we need give our attention.

And thus it is no accidental lapse of artistic momentum that causes the author to veer off the direct path of the story and lead us through the flea market where Julius buys the old field glasses to help in his nocturnal observations. Again we are asked to stroll, this time through that "way station for migratory souls," and look at an old porcelain figurine of Venus, which, like the field glasses, has its own story and its own memories of another time and place and its long-dead owner. The things we see are not just objects; they are the repositories of what is warm, human, and sometimes heroic, even long after their human creators or owners are themselves gone. We owe them our thoughtful reverence; and it matters not at all whether we know their actual history or invent one for them — even that act of falsification is a human and humanizing activity if done with some warmth and affection. Moreover, things have feelings, souls: the narrator likens the human feeling of uselessness to the sensation a door must have when it's taken off its hinges and leaned against a wall; and Dr. Döblinger claims that even rocks have souls — they just move very much more slowly than the rest of us. But, if we close ourselves to the mystery, the aura, the associations, and regard each of the treasures we come across as mere objects, we bring on the darkness, as Julius does when he utters the word "object" to describe a woman he's observing. In fact, Doderer allows us to test the thesis for ourselves: by having Julius use the totally objective descriptor "blue-green" in designating a certain star, both we and Julius fail to make the myriads of subjective, mythologic, and literary associations that go with the name "Venus," which that star most surely is — as Julius eventually discovers and ends upon the floor amongst the wreckage of his "scientific" equipment. All of which makes understandable the narrator's oft-repeated mantra; "but those things are basically just trivialities, anyway." Nothing could be further from the truth: those not so trivial things and feelings are the entryways to life; those living bits of the past are the elements from which we ought to assemble our futures, and they supply, in addition, warmth with which to face what may seem like a cold existence. The narrator has been putting us on, challenging us to disprove him.

To approach the reader's second question: the complexity of the language, somewhat unusual even for Doderer, results from its being tied to the thoughts and actions of both narrator and hero. For instance, the rascally narrator gets himself all tied up in a never-ending sentence he's using to describe the runaround being given to some poor soul who's come to the tax office to make an inquiry. Quite frequently, in fact, the narrator's sentences are so long that he has to start them over to get himself back on track — even he seems to have been infected by the byzantine language of the frequent excerpts from the Civil Service Administrative Practices Manual, which is the only book that Julius has ever read since his student days. It is a book that exemplifies the "bad kind of history" — detailed, profuse, logical, joyless, inhuman; but nonetheless, it reflects the sort of safe haven offered by orderliness and predictability.

Julius' words consistently reflect that fact that he is a bureaucrat through and through even in his retirement. The language with which he ruminates about his nocturnal activities — the simple, straightforward act of voyeurism — is hyperbolic as well as pedantically bureaucratic, not only making much out of little, but also blowing great obfuscatory clouds around his base activities, obscuring them from himself as well as — he hopes — from the reader. And his antagonist in the duel of the voyeurs, the slithery Herr Wänzrich (whose name, by the way, means something like "buggy") is an equally comic master of obscuring what he's really saying. Cut from the same cloth, just decorated differently, the two are prime examples of the way people use language dishonestly and that dishonesty, stands out clearly when their words are contrasted with the simple, direct, sometimes lyrical way the author describes landscapes, cityscapes, and the warmer, human relationships between Julius and his friends.

If this were the sum total of the language problem, it would remain simply humorous, like the pompous descriptions of Zihal's new telescope, his highly organized deliberations about how to set it up, and his outlining things in his head under "a" and "b" as if he were thinking in "inter-office memoese." Much worse, however, this unceasing drive to organize and codify — which is what rationalism may degenerate into — can really take over one's thought processes, much the same way a horror-film "alien" takes over one's body, and then readily inflict itself on other subjects, not merely "the usual" ones — in this instance, the daily affairs of the Tax Office. That this process has ominous undertones is hinted at by Julius' easy and frequent alternation between the bureaucratic and martial idioms and also by the "anger that knew no bounds" which came over him when Herr Wänzrich ultimately refused to fit into his scheme of things.

Worse yet, the organizational principle can be put to use in the services of terror, as the narrator points out: ". . . man endures ordered terror more easily and patiently, even though, basically, it may be much more frightful than terror without order . . ." And with that thought we have arrived at an Adolf Eichmann, the bureaucrat as beast, whose actions are divorced from any moral consideration, concerned solely with organization and logistics, and cloaked in a "neutral," circumlocutory, evasive, dishonest administrative language that has been called the "lingua tertii imperii." While one might wonder whether the line quoted above was a postwar insight, or even an opportunistic revision of the manuscript by Doderer, this is what he wrote in his diary in 1940, not long after *The Lighted Windows* had been pretty much completed: ". . . the devil [is] the mirror image of the intellect; psychological mechanisms work in entirely the same way whether propelled by this impetus or that one . . . just as a horse's gallop is always the same whether it happens to be carrying a hero into battle or rescuing a coward from it — that's just the way horses gallop and the rider rides the same way in both cases." And: "Firmly planted there already, devised according to the new coordinates, is the cross, and hanging on it is a body, martyred by the demons of order."

Fortunately our Julius is spared this fate. The world more or less inflicts itself on him, "swirling the freshness of the outside world into the inner" through his eyes, first in the guise of the accidentally seen naked women, then in the form of friendship with the warm, bosomy Rosl Oplatek, not to mention the assaulting of his other senses by the caressing, floating cobwebs and breezes of Indian summer. His attempts to put the world, especially the world of Eros, into a file are in vain. Throw in a few catastrophes precipitated by Zihal's failing to see danger because he's so obsessed with small details and add a bit of adroit staging by his housekeeper, Frau Zadichek (can there be some hidden message in the saving of this Austrian bureaucrat by ladies with Bohemian names?) and voila! Julius is rescued, doubtless by matrimony sometime after the story ends with Rosl going off to see Mozart's *Magic Flute*, that most wonderful of operas which contains the aria "Man und Weib und Weib und Mann, reichen an die Gottheit an." ("Man and woman together come close to the divine.") Doderer has provided a comically archetypical ending for a story set in a country that had gained more through marriage than war.

In fairness to Julius, not all of his humanization is gained passively or by chance. Though at first he attempts to reject or suppress the siren call of memory and the senses, the growing influence of Eros makes him more and more receptive and after the final catastrophe of sorts — the wreck of his "observatory" — he rises to human stature as he turns his back on the wreckage and takes a giant step for his personal humanity by turning on the light. Human status, with its chaos and risks, is finally achieved only after the fall of the bureaucrat. Until that point, however, he has not been the one who has thrown the switch, so to speak. The "stars" in the heaven that confront and ultimately humanize him take on light by themselves, confronting Julius with a whole series of epiphanies — fleshly ones at that — in the original sense of the word.

Little of Zihal's transformation from troglodyte to human seems to be the result of introspection or self-energized psychological insight, however. Everything starts with the outside world, with external appearances and then leads inward, almost reminiscent of Conrad's writings. In fact, all references to what might be called modern psychology are farcical ones: the outlandish phallic symbolism of Julius' probing eyeballs and his telescope is made abundantly clear; his "split personality," alternating in Jekyll-Hyde fashion between nocturnal voyeurism and a Biedermeier daytime existence, is described literally as a "board partition running across his body;" and his superego is cast as the glowering imperial Double Eagle that admonishes him in his fevered dreams during the psychosomatic collapse that follows his being caught at his nasty, nighttime activities. In general, Doderer had little good to say for psychiatry and psychiatrists, whom he once called "Garagists" — auto mechanics, in other words — of the psyche. If there was a saving grace in Julius, it had less to do with insight and more to do with some slight capacity to view things with a tinge of irony. Irony and humor, the banes of ideologues.

In the end, one might be tempted, particularly given the references to Goethe's *Faust* , to view Julius' escapades as merely a satirical contribution to the long line of Germanic ruminations on the theme of nature vs. intellect. However, it may well be closer to the truth to regard the entire tale as the author's assertion of Vienna's baroque heritage, with its religious, mystical, and emotional overtones, against the rationalism of the enlightenment, the perverted end-product of which is not the man who explores and understands everything, but the man who classifies and orders everything while truly understanding very little and who ends up being dehumanized in the process. Doderer's technique, the density of his prose, the flood of images and visual metaphors in the current work are nothing if not baroque: the wavering progression of the narrative itself is like a baroque column, with all those undulations, swirls, and florid decorations that capture the eye, and perhaps ultimately part of the soul, as it ascends to full height. And all the little hints point in that direction, too: the sentences that start over again like the *da capo* of the recitative in baroque opera; the descriptions of Rosl Oplatek sitting in her Junoesque clouds like so many of those opulent, cloud-surrounded ladies that adorn the ceilings of Vienna's baroque town palaces; the sunbeams that traverse Zihal's windows and alight at just the right spot, just the way they pierce the dome of St. Charles Church and strike the eye of God above the altar and are imitated over and over again by those gilded, baroque, sunbursts carved in wood that surround countless mirrors and adorn countless walls in Vienna. Looked at another way, Doderer has sided, whether or not by conscious design, against the views of his father and his modernist colleagues and with older spirits such as the architect Gottfried Semper, who claimed that ". . . the haze of carnival candles is the true atmosphere of art." Or to put it in words from the novel, ". . . nothing that is observed in broad daylight is as captivating as that which takes place behind a window pane . . . illuminated by candles."

After this book, like his creation Julius Zihal, who has evolved and left his solitary moth's burrow to enter life with all its disorderliness "on two, three, or even more tracks," Doderer himself would soon take the evolutionary step into novelistic "polyphony instead of a single voice." Henceforth, especially in the two later novels, *The Strudelhof Staircase* and *The Demons*, which established his reputation as one of Austria's most important twentieth-century writers, the author would no longer "hide behind Julius Zihal," but reach far beyond the size and scope of the more or less "biographical" *Lighted Windows*. His future novels would encompass many Viennese lives, some related to each other, some isolated, some at cross purposes, some living in concert, and some that would open into more splendid creatures, like butterflies emerging. But their literary creator would never fail to pause and reverence the spirits that live in small things — a bear rug, a lamp — nor fail to hear the song of the harp in places as unlikely as the overhead wire stroked by the trolley. He would attempt to describe and understand the fabric of life by examining the long, intersecting courses of individual threads, admitting that his characters' stories had begun before he wrote them down and would continue after his novel ended. So: with that kind of writing, perhaps a late-blooming modern after all? Is that, after all, the proper category in which to file Doderer? But wait: standing off to the side is the new, humanized Julius, shaking his head disapprovingly at the very question, fearing that we have missed the point — about ourselves as well as about literature.

ACKNOWLEDGMENTS AND NOTES

As a sort of posthumous joke, Doderer, who died in 1966, forces the translator into petty bureaucratic behavior, making him list and index the various recurring phrases to be sure that they have been translated identically each time. Hence it is an admission of an only slightly wider Zihaloid streak to confess to having consulted the "Dienstpragmatik," the old Austro-Hungarian "Handbook of Administrative Practices" to see whether Doderer actually quoted the various paragraphs or invented them. The several passages found in the editions of the handbook made available by Ms. Silke Sahl of the Harvard Law Library are identical to Doderer's text, so there is very good reason to assume that the remainder are actual quotations from some other repository of that dreadful, administrative prose.

Prof. Peter Bien provided the original Greek derivation of the word "epiphany" as well as the information that "Bilitis" (p. 107) was supposedly an ancient Greek poetess, a contemporary of Sappho on Lesbos, though she may have been totally the invention of the late nineteenth-century Frenchman who "translated" her works. Dr. K. Seil of Swarovski Optik, Tirol, supplied valuable facts about the history of field glasses and binoculars and pointed out that "Trieder" (p. 68) were binoculars designed to be quickly field-stripped for cleaning.

Finally, I am indebted to the nameless bureaucrat of the I.R.S. who authored the form letter I received while working on the translation. That letter convinced me that the standard for rendering the excerpts from the "Dienstpragmatik" into English should be that after five or six consecutive readings they ought to begin to make a kind of sense. Just barely. Seen in that light, Doderer's novel is indeed quite contemporary.

John S. Barrett

The subtitle of this story may appear at first sight to imply a sort of insult to the honor of the bureaucracy and to be carrying, as poorly concealed contraband, what amounts to nothing less than torpedoes with which the writer (and the nastiness of such people is notorious) is about to attack the honor of the bureaucracy. However, I can prove that it's the readers, or better said, the listeners, who are doing the torpedoing, caught in the very act by the beam of my policeman's flashlight (because we literary folk are the real policemen) which is illuminating an anarchical interior, a — truly! — torpedoed imperial and royal Habsburg civic interior. If one is, of course, immediately receptive to such things and prepared to believe them! Oh, I see that tiny crack in your soul through which the worm of indignation has slithered in, and if I didn't have to be afraid of being taken to task by knowledgeable people for a somewhat forced metaphor, I would say "the whispering worm" and nothing more.

Et quid susurrant vermes? What are those motile, sophistic little heads whispering? They're saying, "If a bureaucrat has to become a human being at some point, what can he have been before that, other than a beast?"

Just as if, for example, there was no such thing as a fallen angel.

This angel fell when he was pensioned. He fell from the abstract heights of suprapersonal authority directly into an empty space, into a sort of intermediate realm, that no man's land which separates a mystical, or at least mysterious, government agency from life and ordinary human beings, from whom it remains isolated in a vacuum, somewhat like an artist closeted away in the life of l'art pour l'art. And that about sums up, as well, the total lack of contact between the Central Tax Assessment Office and the ordinary common-sense folk subject to it. It simply assessed according to its own standards of assessment, which were taken from its own, completely autonomous regulations. Whoever might actually go looking for some rhyme or reason there would stand convicted — first of all by virtue of his feebleness of mind for having simply gotten all those regulations mixed up; second, because of his lack of appreciation for history — which is revealed by his inability to arrive at a clear concept of the baroque way of life; and thirdly, he would stand convicted by revealing in broad daylight his totally vulgar turn of mind — in regard to sublime matters, to put it simply, you don't just come right out with such brazen and dumb questions.

Incidentally, a word has been let fall here which is of eminent significance for Zihal's biography, namely, "concept." He had succeeded, you see, somewhere around the thirtieth year of his life, in arriving at a concept. Oh! Now I'm going to be understood in a profane way again, not at all suited to those heights where angels live — before their fall. Perhaps at the mention of the words "arriving at a concept," you might think of some sort of overview, a plan for one's life, a getting-things-straight on Zihal's part, for instance, about the way in which he ought to arrange his life and other trivialities of that sort (well, what else but trivialities . . . ?). No, what we're talking about here amounts to a hierarchical formulation, really . . . A "manipulant," an assistant, later and semi-officially called a "practicant," or trainee . . . well, those are little mice. The church mice of the hierarchy, faces that look like they've been pressed flat when seen on the street, under the beams of the arc lights. Passers-by, nothing more. This is what it says about them in the addendum to §57, concluding paragraph, of the Handbook of Administrative Practices of the Civil Service:

> "Practicants who, on February 1, 19 hundred so-and-so, after the exclusion of time spent in active military service (excluded according to §30 of the HAP) have already served the requisite time for promotion within the same branch of said department (§56) and have

passed the required special examination in a way reflecting a satisfactory level of qualification, will be — unless there exists a legal reason for exclusion or some other hindrance — designated, effective 1 February 19 hundred so-and-so, as Civil Servants of the *lowest* rank in the Civil Service Category under consideration.
Should the duration of service completed by such a practicant within the same branch of the Service, minus time spent in military service (excluded according to §30 of the HAP) which is to be used in the calculation of pension benefits, exceed that necessary for promotion, then the time difference, up to a maximum of four years, will be *credited* as extra service time, to be included at the next higher salary level."

On the other hand, an "Officiant" — a clerk, really — is already someone to be addressed as if he were a human being. But the vowel "a" only gets to be pronounced as a long "a" when it comes to an "Official." It is, to be sure, only the beginning of a certain latitude, the beginning letter of a broader sort of life, where one gets to sit behind a desk. And then one could even get to be a "Senior Official" — a life fulfilled.

But who succeeds — and how does he — in propelling his life into another dimension, out of the flattened planimetry of the lowest step, out of the ordinary office job — and into the realm of concepts, into stereometry, where he can "arrive at a concept," become an official whose duties deal with concepts, and consecrate himself to a higher calling and thus bring forth fruit from nobler seed?

The people who succeeded were the ones who took a "pressure-cooker" course (yes, that's what it was called back in those dim, dark times when Zihal was alive) and, somewhat soggy but nevertheless properly cooked as far as education was concerned, were able to pass the "Intelligence Test." That's what it was called, quite shamelessly; their degree of intelligence was questioned, directly and openly — in the rawest way, one might say — because otherwise it would not have been tested.

But that was just a symbol. Even in higher cultures there are relatively crude symbols: one only need think about the public consummation of royal marriages and such like, which would certainly have caused indignation even on Zihal's part, had they come to his attention; but immodest details of that sort were not to be found among the historical ingredients that went into the pressure-cooker course.

2

He became a Revisor, responsible for overseeing and correcting the reports of his subordinates.

It would be natural to think that Zihal might have revised the past, subjected it to a revision at such an abrupt bend in the meandering stream of life, instead of hovering so indecisively in the new sphere, indeed with a matter-of-factness that almost borders on defiance here — one might call it that, but we're really not inclined to, because despite all the aggravation he causes us, somehow we still like Zihal. That he hovered makes sense. He had indeed become more weighty in the sense of importance, but had lost weight in the earth-specific sense. You have to imagine him this way: as a man who had succeeded in swallowing a small gas-filled balloon . . . Furthermore, that buoyancy allowed Zihal — in the epoch between his having become a Revisor and when he became a Senior Revisor — to go floating off into the heaven of his first marriage. To say more about that at this point is not really possible, although later, as a widower, Zihal did just that, willingly and frequently, especially in the company of a certain Doctor Döblinger, a person who was quite adept at opening the sluice gates of Zihalistic loquaciousness with cleverly placed leading questions and then sinking the net of his attention, so to speak, into the flood of conversation, thus to fish out many details — not always nice ones . . . far too many details, I should say; and with that I've already indicated the reason why I neither can nor care to relate anything about Zihal's first marriage (he almost always used to start with the words "My first wife was eighteen years older than I") other than this one thing: that years later, the Councillor Julius

Zihal came home from his wife's funeral just as little changed as did Zihal, the Revisor, when he returned from the honeymoon trip that took him as far as Paris — which at first might sound surprising and almost unbelievable . . . but which is easily explained and legitimized by the not unfavorable financial circumstances of Frau Anna Deidosik — which was the name of Zihal's first wife, herself a widow. Women are, of course, always more eager to be doing things than men. Back then, postcards from Paris fell like hailstones onto various befriended desks at the Central Tax Assessment Office, and even dropped on a nearby inn, and at the Café Simberl, which, in honor of the aforementioned office, had actually introduced an original, reduced-price combination for the afternoon coffee break (the "Tax Office Refresher," coffee topped with whipped cream and two pieces of crumb cake) — anyway, at Café Simberl those cards were pinned up by the cash register, so that the first thing the regular patrons came across was the news from Julius Zihal.

3

The times were hardly favorable for an out-of-office revision. You have to imagine your way back into those circumstances, so foreign to us today because we've long since progressed beyond them. It was a dark and gloomy time that might still have been named for that notorious, old, Chancellor of the State, who was long dead even then: the Era of Metternich. And with that, everything becomes more or less understandable. Even that puzzling Central Tax Office. Everyone seemed to exude a gelatinous sort of humanity, people took their opinions and any other bits of unpleasantness out onto the street for a walk without the least embarrassment, something they do today only with their dogs. But no one really bothered about those opinions or convictions; they were simply ignored. They hardly ever made it into conversation and certainly never into real discussion. It was suppression of the worst sort. As soon as someone got up on his high horse about some conviction or other he promptly slid off again, mostly out of laziness, but sometimes because it just got too boring sitting up there without anyone listening or paying any attention to him. Common sense indulged in virtual orgies and its platitudes were not uncommonly presented — by Zihal's lips, for instance — on a bed of sonorous tone and decorum. It was just such a tone that the previously mentioned Doctor Döblinger so splendidly knew how to elicit from Zihal by abruptly confronting him with some generalization like "True universal education never imparts dead knowledge" — which would provoke Zihal to state some all-encompassing viewpoint with an assurance that was astonishing, and which, indeed, could even generate something in the listener that I might be tempted to designate paradoxically as — home-sickness. At least that's what I've often felt. For the most part, he used to answer by defining things — in other words, almost like a Cardinal. He'd begin with a counter-question, such as, "What do you mean by 'dead knowledge?'" And from there: "Herr Doctor, you, as an academically educated person . . ." and here one could see that this was somehow a sore spot for Zihal, probably due to the fact that his intelligence had been tested (because of the "pressure-cooker" course) but also because he certainly didn't want to have knowledge in general designated as dead, since it really had helped him from one level of life to a different one . . . Once he even defined the concept of "literature" in a similar way and I made a mental note of that definition: "What does 'literature' mean? Herr Doctor! You'll pardon me, of course, you being an academically educated person, all to your credit, as you well know. But I am a serious person. And I don't read novels. Literature, for me, is something one Jew writes about another one."

Later it came out that that definition wasn't even his, but instead, the pronouncement of a very well known politician of the time, and besides that, it was intended by the latter as an explanation of the word "science," which of course amounts to a considerable difference.

4

The bureaucrat moved into a new apartment after his retirement. You can visualize the whole thing: scarcely released from the sacred precincts and already he's being intruded upon by the profane, the incidental, in short, by private life. To be sure, this still took, to a certain extent, the form of a file being closed; however, that form was no longer identical with its content — a concept which, in the Central Tax Assessment Office just as in the world of art, belonged to the category of the completely obvious, for the precise reason that every matter that was taken up there was immediately and completely separated from life and its chaotic lack of quality on one hand and from its mundane-purposeful order on the other, specifically, at that moment which I'd like to term "becoming a file." A file has, in a certain sense, an existence that is just as independent and separated from the rest of the world as a work of art; and those splendid lines of Eduard Mörike are every bit as applicable to a file:

> *"Every genuine work of art*
> *reveals its bliss within itself."*

Mörike, of course, had not been left out when it came to a literary education sufficient to the intelligence test; and indeed you might also say that there was absolutely nothing about that poet which could cause moral reservations. Unfortunately, with newer authors that's not exactly the usual case.

Yes, that giant Antaeus-Zihal, who had so often drawn himself up to an impressive height behind his desk — the entire man (physically he had, in fact, ended up rather short) merely a part of that insurmountable wall of current regulations which acted as a barrier to any party lodging a complaint or hoping to speed up some process — so as to refer the petitioner to room 289, third floor, for the purpose of exercising his legal right to have his appeal heard (where he would, of course, be immediately referred to room 12, mezzanine, the appeals office for those who had failed to file on time) — yes, I know this sentence is getting to be as endless as those long corridors in the Central Tax Assessment Office — anyway, that giant Antaeus — to get back to him as well as the person running around in the corridors, who, in the end, was

sent back to Zihal again by the people in room 12 — was actually
the person who had jurisdiction over such matters . . .

It doesn't happen that way; you get out of breath in those
endless corridors.

And all I'd really wanted to say was that the physically rather
short, retired bureaucrat Julius Zihal was simply no longer the
giant Antaeus and had lost the ground under his feet as he
awakened in bed at seven o'clock one spring morning in the year
nineteen hundred so-and-so, wearing his moustache trainer — on
the day before he'd been to the office for the last time — and
immediately made an attempt to preserve his previous inner
attitude, by trying to make even the matter of moving to a different
apartment take on the form of opening a new file. And in that way
he ran into trouble; the unity of content and form — back there, in
the building of 1000 rooms and 1000 labyrinths, the easiest thing
in the world to achieve — could not be achieved here, on this
ground. Zihal, who was still half asleep, experienced something
like a mild shock. We assume that this shock resulted basically
from the purposeful-mundane quality of the impending action,
which now shoved itself into Zihal's imagination like a blunt
wedge. As a musical accompaniment, the hoarse, grumbling noise
of the coffee grinder started up in the kitchen at the same moment,
muted by the intervening walls, indicating that his housekeeper had
let herself in with her key and was now preparing the morning
coffee out there.

And she was the one who, at the very outset, simply brushed
aside Zihal's attempt to give form to the situation as an un-
necessary complication. The bureaucrat complied. Because Frau
Zadichek was to continue to preside over her areas of jurisdiction
in his life. Zihal's already chosen, new living quarters were located
only a few streets away, in the same neighborhood; indeed the
distance his housekeeper had to travel there turned out to be
somewhat shorter.

Even though, as far as she was concerned, she'd like to have
gotten the bureaucrat out of the way — and soon, since she was
supposed to get started packing that very morning — she still

could not prevent him . . . from calculating.

Because, despite his secret decision to stay in bed somewhat longer in order to enjoy this sabbath melancholy in the middle of the week, on a workday morning — something which would absolutely never again dawn for him — Zihal got up at the usual time anyway, hung his moustache trainer on a little nail that had been driven into the curved wood of the headboard near the night table for that purpose, slid into his socks, bedroom slippers, and trousers and began to shave next to the window, in front of a small mirror that was hanging at a jaunty angle from the latch. Presently he stood in front of the iron wash stand, snorting and puffing. The section of the wall directly behind it had been sensibly covered with oilcloth to resist the spray. The purpose and utility of the wash stand had been complemented by several small, equally sensible excrescences along the edge of the oilcloth, such as the holder for the moustache brushes which looked out from a sort of pocket which had the amusing overall shape of a knitted bedroom slipper. Even elsewhere the furniture had an influence on the walls directly behind, as if by radiation: above the head end of the bed, Our Lady of Maria Zell guarded the bureaucrat's sleep from within her dark, elliptical frame, while on the long wall, somewhat astonishingly, hung something rosy pink on which a forest nymph could be seen in front of a pond, hovered about by little fairies; but completely and entirely clothed was something that the nymph was not. The desk in the adjoining room — there were two rooms plus the kitchen in front — had also projected something onto the wall, namely a calendar (from the grocer's where Frau Zadichek did the shopping for the official, handed out on New Year's); but first and foremost, right in the middle, the Monarch, in the form of a framed and glass-covered reproduction of the portrait by Pochwalsky, which, as everyone knows, is the truest to life of all those in existence (in his Styrian hunting outfit with a dead stag at his feet).

Actually we wanted to talk about calculating, the thing which Frau Zadichek was not able to prevent the official from doing. But the path to calculating is more than calculating, the way to the desk is more than the desk (a variation on a theme by the most famous of the newer German poets, who certainly must have known that just from his external resemblance to Goethe) — but that way to the desk, in other words, to calculating, was now immoderately shortened, amputated and hacked off as it were, because it now led merely through the next room and not even to a desk but into the kitchen where Zihal was accustomed to drinking his coffee. In passing, he took along several expired and torn-off pages of the wall calendar, which he used to save so he could use their empty back sides, as well as a pencil, then sat down, stirred, slurped, and broke his breakfast roll.

That all moves are divided into three parts is beyond any doubt and that's something they have in common with the movements of a sonata, for example. To be more precise, one can distinguish: first, moving out; second, the act of moving; third, moving in. Assuming, of course, that the reason for moving to a new apartment is firmly and properly grounded. This previously driven-in nail is what the official now examined again. The reason for moving was to be seen, in this instance, in the difference which had arisen between the salary drawn while in active service and the retirement benefits which pertained henceforth, said decrease in the household budget to be equalized by the decrease in the rent, thanks to the lower price of the new apartment; at which point, there even remained a small surplus. Regarding the disposal of the new level of income that began to flow in, so to speak, on a monthly basis, the bureaucrat was still reserving decision, though the latter (namely, the decision) had already been oriented in a certain direction, of course, by virtue of the tripartite moving expenses that were about to result. The figures confirmed that there was no need to dip into the interest on the Deidosik estate — somewhat higher than Zihal's pension — that is, if the considerations taken into account at this point remained valid, both with respect to the amount that could be reasonably expended for general living expenses as well as that to be set aside from the very same monthly income and put into a savings account. At the same time, a new, somewhat tighter household budget was envisioned. With all that, however, the reason for moving was deemed to be properly grounded. In the matter at hand, difficulties now presented themselves, mainly in respect to a more precise elucidation of how the costs should be allotted. If the boxes which had to be made were to be charged, without further consideration, to "moving out" — because they were a prerequisite for packing up — then the bill from the moving company, agreed upon and expected momentarily, belonged just as much to that entry as to either of the two following categories. The tip for the movers themselves could be listed under the heading "moving in," since it would have to be given only after the furniture had actually been delivered and put in place. The final tip for the concierge of the old building was obvious because of its "moving out" character. "Moving itself" remained free of charges not attributable to either the first or third categories.

Yes, really, he struggled to achieve form, he felt momentarily very close to the act of becoming a file — close to order achieved in the sole possible way, to decorum, which, in Zihal, swelled in pomp and dignity like a trumpet's note. And so it asserted itself once again, the tax office. But a blunt, gray wedge broke in from the side, just as Phillip's phalanx did against the serried rows of the Hellenes once upon a time. There the burden of earthly things grew, there content spilled over, with its sad formlessness and formless sadness.

Because dividing up his belongings, the packing of such very different things into boxes, trunks, baskets, bags — *that* had no intention of giving birth on its own to a principle of form. If one, for example, postulated a basic difference between clothing and underwear, shoes, utilitarian articles and articles that weren't actually used — for instance that (rosy pink) picture above the bed — where, now, should one put the things for the shoes, namely the things for polishing shoes, the brushes, the rags, the little applicators, the round cans with polish or creme . . . and where does the wedding picture of his dead parents go? . . . and the bucket? Yes, where? A bucket — perhaps it shouldn't even be packed at all! And . . . what would that look like? Like a bunch of gypsies. Noise everywhere, all the pots and pans in the kitchen yelling out curtly and rudely like some mob of people who make their threatening presence known in that way; everything was making noise out there — in just one small spot the tin wastebasket, the short broom with its bobbed head, and a half-hidden bucket that was standing there holding left-over shreds from the grater, all banging, scraping, and clanging as if they were announcing their presence. In such fashion the bureaucrat's consciousness, which usually encompassed only what was close at hand and, above all, respectable, was struck by all that forgotten junk — so necessary even in a bachelor's home — which, just standing there, was hardly noticeable, or just familiar or pleasant, but now was behaving like a band of dervishes, not subject to any order, not walking one in front of the other in an orderly procession, but making a mockery of the tripartite form of the sonata. And then, it was just at that point that the bureaucrat fell into Frau Zadichek's arms, only figuratively of course and in another category from that of the moral or immoral, because actually he fell into her hands, in the sense of "falling into the hands of thieves." The last remnants of his desire for form came crashing down onto the quivering and crumbling ground of his bewilderment; and later, when he appeared in the doorway, bent as if under a yoke, Frau Zadichek realized that her moment had come and it wasn't even necessary for the official to make mention — out of a deeper malaise which certainly would have been incomprehensible to his housekeeper — of the chaos that had broken out in the affairs of his home! . . . "No need t'get upset, the Herr Councillor doesn't need t'worry about a thing, he can just take a little walk over to the coffee house and read the paper, nothing's gonna get broken because I'm packing all the dishes and things separately, some goes into the clothes hamper, the glasses I'm stuffing with socks, and the wash basin and pitcher and all the rest go in with the bedding."

He'd managed to forget the things on the wash stand entirely. But they were just something extra, they just fell on top of everything else and didn't break; but something else did, namely, inside Julius Zihal. He walked into the kitchen again, this time to really get his hat and coat and leave. A narrow sunbeam was coming through the window, straight as an arrow, aimed at the little box with the shoe things, that is, the things for polishing shoes, the brushes, the rags, the round cans of polish . . . one was standing upright, like a disc, a black background with yellow writing around the edge and a picture of the heel of a shoe in the middle, a rubber heel, recommended and praised by the advertisement. Under the gaze of the sun, however, that can of polish took on an entirely different meaning than the one it had revealed to Zihal's eyes, roving around uncertainly as they were in hopes of finding the formal principal of packing. The precise meaning which had been intended by the can was: shoe polish and an advertisement for rubber heels — nothing else. Now, however, it meant a distinct landscape in very close proximity to Vienna. There was a valley, with a road leading down into it, and as it fell away toward the city, it was like a blue, already shadowed tongue licking between the vineyards that lay there under the hesitant, ponderous sun of the late afternoon and early evening, with contours that seemed to drip gold, almost as if the mountain were pouring forth our local wine directly, without vintner, without harvest, without press. And that gold extended down into the valley as far as a small stone house, whose windowless rear wall praised, in monstrous black with gigantic yellow lettering — and with the picture of the heel in the middle! — the same object that the small polish can did, just in a larger format. All of that, however, was driven gold-green into the bureaucrat's interior by the well-aimed sunbeam, as if it were a sharp wedge. He saw himself walking down into the valley there, warmed by the wine, past the little stone house, plunging into the cool, licking tongue of the valley that now was sinking from blue into gray just exactly the way one exhaled the last warmth, that golden mountain within one's self lent by the wine, the beautiful view, the conversation — and then walking on to the nearby streetcar terminus, in order to doze off in some corner, found by luck despite all the dust and crowds.

And so it rose up again — the tax office "youth," that is, or

whatever you want to call it, because basically such things are just
trivialities, anyway; and as such the Herr Councillor wanted to
push such foolishness aside, get the bell of the trumpet open so to
speak, so that the sound within it could swell in dignity and
decorum. But it didn't work. The tone broke, it "squawked," as
musicians say. And the bureaucrat gave a helpless, but sour, smile.
He looked out of the kitchen window, one of the many kitchen
windows in the neighborhood decorously covered by small curtains; on the window, chives were propped in a small glass of
water to stay fresh; propped behind them was a day finally making
itself known with a definite light in which the familiar, fragmented
line of houses, roofs, and the opposite street corner were asserting
themselves. Julius Zihal finally shrugged his shoulders. That was
his last weapon, an effective one. And then he went to Café
Simberl, in keeping with Frau Zadichek's wishes, which for the
bureaucrat, without the latter's having been entirely conscious of
the facts of the matter, presented the sole legitimization for
something as outlandish as sitting in a café in the morning. It was
balmy in the street, surprisingly warmer than in the apartment —
a dawn, a beginning that would not let itself be avoided. And a
beginning justified by the pronouncement of Frau Zadichek. In the
café, Zihal sat as if he were on a fat, air-filled cushion, as if the
rubber ring which he'd always had on his chair at the tax office
had come along with him invisibly and swelled to four times its
usual size. He slouched toward the glass pane, against which the
sun propped its fingers from the outside. And so they both leaned
against each other, in that balmy and, from the moral standpoint,
not always irreproachable season.

5

The bureaucrat's new apartment was located in a curiously
narrow wing of a tall building, on the fourth floor in fact, with two
rooms and a kitchen as before, but with all three rooms behind one
another — on a single axis, as people used to say. The end room
had two windows opposite each other, so that there was a view
onto different streets, into different zones and configurations of the

tumult of the city's roofs, towards different rows of windows, closed and blindly reflecting or open — and the latter was already quite common now, in the spring. In that room with its view in both directions, one could feel exposed, like an observer sitting in the gondola of a spotting balloon, and the bureaucrat had just that sort of feeling immediately after setting foot in the room for the first time. But soon, after the furniture had been delivered and order prevailed once again in general and in particular, the walls of his dwelling became covered as if by mildew or some film of that sort — by the bureaucrat's radiations. Oilcloth covering, forest nymph, Monarch, and moustache brush all found their places.

Here it was, with those latter arrangements, that the bureaucrat carefully undertook the sole corrections of the Zadichekian dispositions — which, of course, were concerned with life and its necessities on the larger scale. The forest nymph, to take one example, had been hung on somewhat of a slant. The tear-off calendar from the grocer was hanging off center in relation to the desk, quite far to the right; but the bureaucrat left it unaltered — any intervention would have been too obvious and almost somewhat of a reprimand. In the kitchen which now, finally, contained only things which had been taken care of and put in order, he caught sight of the little box with the things for polishing shoes. It was sitting there in the pale shaft of sunlight coming in through the window. The yellow polish can with the advertisement of the rubber heel was standing upright again, just as it had before. Zihal, who vaguely sensed impropriety and defiance there, gazed disapprovingly at the state of affairs for several moments, then put the can down flat. Standing there on the table as well were the dishes left over from lunch, which was now being prepared daily in the Zadichek household and brought over for the bureaucrat. An empty beer bottle was within regulations and in keeping with budgetary projections.

He went back into the nearer of his two rooms, where the desk stood, and settled down in front of it. The Handbook of Administrative Practices was quite familiar to him, as was the logical application of the sections relevant to his own case, namely, with respect to the assessment of pension benefits; Zihal had long since, indeed for years, months, and days, subjected all of that to the most exacting scrutiny. It was the addendum to paragraph 57 that was relevant here, particularly subsection c, article III as well as subsection d:

> Should the actual service time under consideration according to §57 sub. b. or c. exceed the pertinent normal duration of service, then the difference *is to be considered* as *E x c e s s   S e r v i c e   T i m e* (Total Excess Service Time, Prior Excess Service Time, etc.) — up to a maximum of four years, however — and will be *c r e d i t e d* toward the advancement to the next higher salary category.
> As a result of that *c r e d i t*, the Civil Service Officer, in so far as he has not yet completed the service time interval necessary for promotion from his current rank classification, *is to be considered* as having spent the Excess Service Time (to a maximum of four years), as well as the already completed portion of the service time necessary for promotion, at his current rank; however, in so far as the Excess Service Time credit (to a maximum of four years) has not been completely used up in this way, he *is to be considered* as already having spent the remaining portion of same at the salary of the next higher rank classification. A Civil Service Officer who on 1 February 19. . has already completed the service time necessary for promotion from the salary category of his rank, is, by virtue of amassed credit, *to be considered* as having already spent the entire Excess Service Time (to a maximum of four years, however) in the salary category of the next higher rank classification.

Addendum to §57, sub. d.

> The determination of whether, and to what extent, prior Excess Service Time is to be credited to a Civil Service Officer who on 1 February 19 . . occupies the h i g h-

e s t rank and salary category which can be attained through promotion by virtue of service time, as well as accrual, through Excess Service Time, of credit for advancement to a higher salary level in that same rank classification, is to be carried out in analogous fashion to cases treated under §57 sub. c.

In this instance, such a Civil Service Officer is *to be considered* as having spent, in addition to the already completed portion of the service time required for advancement of salary level, the Excess Service Time (four years maximum) receiving wages of his current salary level; however, in so far as the Excess Service Time credit (maximum four years) has not been used up in this way, *he is to be considered* as having already completed the remaining portion of same receiving the wages of the next higher salary level.

The latter regulation had found application in Zihal's case and things had come to a favorable conclusion. He felt himself summarized and substantiated in the most exacting way. And that was necessary and it made him feel good. Because, with all of that, his mood while he was sitting there at the desk was like a trouser button that had come loose and was hanging by a thread. The thin spring sun slanted through the room, the rumbling of distant vehicles sounded, one might well say, not self-assured enough when heard from there; indeed, it had the slightly unpleasant after-effect of indistinctly spoken words that now made their way to the vulnerable, exposed Julius Zihal, who no longer felt the all-powerful, reprimanding, praising, or approving weight of office behind him. A small point of contention was therefore welcome. Zihal had, in fact, had to come up with the cost of moving on his own, as a private person, no longer someone on active duty who's being transferred to another office, for instance; and thus he was certainly not entitled to enjoy certain perquisites as set forth in the supplement to §58 of the Handbook of Administrative Practices:

Travel expense allowances (tickets, meals, and lodging)

are determined by the rank category in which the Civil
Service Officer was last listed.

In contradistinction, the furniture allowance (§ *3 of The
Regulations Concerning Change of Dwelling of 13
September 1804*) is to be based on the most recent
salary level; and the highest level of rent allowance (§
68 HAP) on the prevailing level of activity, even if the
Officer has reached the pertaining benefit levels only
by way of service time credit.

Anger warms one. It is like the tassel on the end of a whip
dangling above the dray-horse of diminishing self confidence. He,
Zihal, had served loyally, for a lifetime, and hadn't attained his
higher salary levels — and thus retirement benefits — by merely
piling up extra time credits. However, regulations are regulations.
He was sitting where he was by the power of precept. To bow
before it imparts greatness. His gaze fell upon the picture of the
Monarch, actually right through it; in his mind, he was taking in
the Double Eagle over the door of the office building. He, Zihal,
was in harmony with it all. His work had not — never — been
found less than satisfactory. There was a slight degree of moistness
around his eyes as he went out to warm up the leftover morning
coffee, because it was time for some refreshment. And suddenly he
was struck by the notion of allowing himself a Virginia afterward.
That was unusual with afternoon coffee. But that's the way it was
going to be, whatever it was that had come over him — grandiose,
to a certain extent, but strangely enough it was consistent with the
place in the Handbook of Administrative Practices where it said,
". . . only after the completion of this calculation can an answer be
given to the question of whether or not total excess service time or
prior excess service time is to be used in determining advancement
based on time served. (§ 57, sub. b. and c.)" Yes, it should be! And
only after the completion of the lighting up ceremony was the
decision going to be made, calmly and in complete contentment,
as to whether or not he'd look up some of his friends from the
Stammtisch — for the first time since he was no longer in active
service — after he'd consumed the supper that was already waiting

in the kitchen cabinet, or whether it might not be better to go right over to Café Simberl, where the whole Stammtisch, including the ladies, used to congregate late in the evening on Thursdays.

The fragrant cloud rose. With it, the first subtle hint of twilight, strangely related to the strong, tropical aroma of the Kaiser-Virginia, in which the Monarch now floated and became indistinct; the little stone house, the one with the black and yellow advertisement down in the shadowed valley, floated and became indistinct, and the sunny, humpbacked hills from which the wine flowed. Finally, something like a residue of all that settled on the floor of the darkening room. And when nothing more floated after it and the darkness became more noticeable, no longer related to the delicious smoke in that dusky way, Julius Zihal turned on the electric light, because he, conscious in his enjoyment, wanted to see the delicious smoke.

6

This time Doctor Döblinger appeared at the Stammtisch almost simultaneously with the bureaucrat, beside whom he immediately took a seat, drawing Zihal into conversation not without enthusiasm, as if the latter had become an entirely new person for him since going into retirement, a person, namely, who has undergone a secret process of transformation and put everything behind him. In that regard, the Doctor — so it appears to us and probably to the reader, too — was not entirely in error; however everything was just barely beginning, at the earliest stage of development. Perhaps the bureaucrat felt something of the sort as well, and thus had dropped that decisively firm, indeed, steely-definitive tone of his, which Herr von Döblinger may have expected to really assert itself after Zihal's career had come to an end and which he therefore may have wanted to bring out.

Only coincidentally did the Cardinal touch upon a subject that had already been treated by that ancient Greek, Plato, in a Socratic dialogue. "What is a citizen?" was the bureaucrat's return question. "Herr Doctor! The goal of a citizen's endeavors should be considered to be the maintenance of the civil servant class in a way befitting its station." However, that sentence seemed to be merely a shield that was held up against Herr Doctor von Döblinger and beneath which a certain slightly sour duplicity was concealed, or more exactly, a certain realization of the fact that, here and now, one was no longer proceeding entirely under the gaze of the Double Eagle, but had actually strayed from the path, and, to be precise, diagonally to the left across the table, where the Post-mistress Rosl Oplatek was sitting. The definition, the effect of which had certainly not been intended by Zihal but was none-theless one of surprise for the Doctor, now created a little space; the interrogator drew back, perhaps because of a kind of lack of air, and Zihal's eye could rest on curves which at the moment, to confess it slightly sourly, concerned him measurably. The curves appeared to be harnessed in green, surmounted by a shock of blond, and legitimized by a face that had no need to shrink from the gaze of the Double Eagle, but nevertheless had to be looked upon and categorized, respectively, as that of what could be called a still rather pretty, respectable, older female person.

Unfortunately the lady had to leave early — she shook hands with Zihal as well and said "Auf Wiedersehen" and "The Herr Councillor should just come again next Thursday!" Later, when they moved over into the café as usual, Zihal took on a certain decorum, namely, by not going along, but, gently and smiling inwardly, turned down what amounted to piling one pleasure on top of another, choosing to be on his way home as an ambulatory picture of moderation. The gates of the buildings were still open. The bureaucrat walked through his own and through the foyer; then, climbing the stairs with the gravity of a person who's carry-ing out a salutary activity at the proper time, he passed by the second and third floors, each of which had its own water faucets on the landing, with fixtures of neatly polished brass that stood out in gleaming contrast and not without a certain ostentatiousness to the gray stone of the well-worn steps when one emerged from the narrow neck of the circular staircase and arrived on the next higher floor. The interior of this building was like the face of a simple, but extremely proper, old woman. Even the little doors which were located next to the entrances of the apartments opposite the stairs presented their coats of brown paint and closed latches with a kind of dignity in those quiet, composed surroundings, even if it was a humanized kind; behind each such door was a short broom with a bobbed head, which at that time had not yet spread over into the world of women's fashion.

Zihal, having arrived on the top floor, put the key to his new apartment to use. Old bachelors enter the anterooms of their homes quite differently from married men, whose asses' ears precede them and are already dangling into the apartment and listening for footsteps, wondering whether *she* is already in bed, or still awake, or whatever else might be going on. It was a long time since such a mechanism within the bureaucrat had shown any sign of movement and far behind was the day when, after his wife's funeral, considering the decorum customarily required at such an affair, he finally got rid of his shoes and coat and stretched out on the divan in the empty apartment with a richly, so to speak, deserved Virginia, something no well-meaning person could have called an excess. We're the only ones who see him lying there now — the windows are standing open because of the warmth, down below the shoemaker's boy is whistling, and still suspended in the next room are the plagiarized chords of a closed chapter in his life, with everything that had been simply left behind by the wife who'd been laid out there and was now buried — furniture pushed together, leftover flowers, and cold candles. We're the only ones who see him lying there now; he himself wasn't thinking of anything at all and his astonished gaze was not falling upon suddenly deepening, illuminated shafts or prism-shaped spaces of the past. That lay behind many crumbling, fissured, little walls, which all together, however — because of the way they'd been put up one behind the other, each extending the other's effect and hiding everything — had the effect of a massive partition wall. It caused him no unease. He took — as if throwing his cape aside while a blaring fanfare announced the next act to a nonexistent audience — a key from the hook and disappeared from the room, feeling his way back through the dark kitchen and then into the next room, toward the desk and then over to the light switch.

By and large it's impossible to say when a so-called historic moment actually arrives, whether or not it's here now, and which of the events that take place is really the decisive one. And, in like fashion, almost everyone goes bumping across his biographical junctions and switches without recognizing them as such; you simply notice the jolting caused by the unevenness. But there was one just now, for Julius Zihal, that is. Facts alone decide, regardless of whether they're visible or invisible and the latter all too soon become accessible to a lens system that is completely physical. The fact which is at issue here is that the bureaucrat, as he was already touching the light switch — and he only failed to press it by an immeasurably fine hair's breadth — that the bureaucrat withdrew his hand again and, without moving a muscle, remained standing in the darkened room, as if he were enclosed in a container, albeit a spacious one, shut away in other words, not really there, standing in that darkness and simultaneously in a piece of time that had stood still, that didn't exist because of the darkness and the complete absence of motion. And perhaps just for that most deeply seated reason, Zihal felt as safe as if he were behind walls and ramparts there. His eyes extended a little beyond them. Yes, we have to say it: he experienced what amounted, first of all, to pleasure, even joy, and his situation consolidated itself to the point that he stroked his moustache in total contentment there in the dark, quite briskly, in the style of one or the other of those dashing, youthful, pre-tax-office gestures (although basically such things were just trivialities). His eyes protruded a little, as if he wanted to decrease as much as possible the distance to what he was looking at, wanted to push or carry his eyeballs even closer to the object that was presenting itself there.

Directly across from him, on the opposite side of one of those narrow alleys where people lived, that grimly impenetrable, traditional arrangement of dark facade and rows of windows was penetrated at a sharply and precisely delineated rectangular area, broken in, to a certain extent, revealing the prism-shaped, bright space of the small room that opened out behind it, which, with its broad, white bed, elicited in the bureaucrat the very strong sensation of something within him standing open, of something tousled and fluffy, perhaps like the down on a goose's belly. Immediately afterward, someone walked in over there. She moved quickly through the room with a light step, a woman in her mid thirties, perhaps, with blond hair that glowed vividly when she stopped for a moment and stood under the electric light in the middle of the room, staring quietly in front of herself. She was wearing long stockings, panties, and camisole, her white arms and shoulders motionless in the light (that was the moment at which the bureaucrat stroked his moustache). She turned briskly toward the bed, sat down on it, leaned forward and pulled off her shoes and stockings. The nightgown descended over her undergarments almost before they were off; she fished the fine, blossom-white things out from under it and off the rug in front of the bed. For a moment she stood and stretched in the long-sleeved gown. Then the light sprang back into itself, as if into its source, and left everything over there mute, empty, and dark — as the bureaucrat went bumping across yet another biographical switch-point. He walked closer to the window, looked to the left, the right, and downward (all the while it was as dark in his head as it was there in the room or in the room across the way after the light had been swallowed up). He was searching around . . . yes . . . for a replacement, for a replacement that would make the light jump into that dark head again, after it had broken another hole in that desolate, dark wall over there; which remained as it was, however — no new lighted, prism-shaped space opened up. Nor did the bureaucrat want to move any closer to the window just then; the one step that he had taken, right after the light had been swallowed up over there, had been taken in fright, chasing the image that had disappeared, so to speak. Now he stood motionless, supported on all sides by the soft upholstery of the dark, in which time stood still, in which he was concealed, hidden, like a tiny moth in a fur deep in a closet. But the second crossover had been traversed, the switch had been thrown, the track changed, and the journey had to continue. It led into the adjoining room, which the bureaucrat reached by feeling his way along without turning on the light. And here were two dark windows pointing in two directions, two dark windows with different views, where here and there (and farther off there and even closer here) the yellowish or whitish, brighter or dimmer constellations of Zihal's newly discovered sky were located — the sick, earthbound stars of the metropolis, which were capable of twinkling just as ambiguously and mysteriously as those in the heavens do. People are always standing in front of windows for a few moments without turning the lights on, "lost in thought" as the saying goes, but the truth is that they're not thinking about anything at all. The same goes for our bureaucrat. His eyes crept forward again, a little closer to the object that he was actually searching for now, for the first time; and with those initial visitations to a horizon of unknown possibilities — which opened up and suddenly became visible from that new apartment, as if the wall obscuring them had collapsed — with those initial visitations, the bureaucrat rumbled unwittingly across the third junction of the evening, traversing a switch that shunted him over onto a completely new, but firmly laid and self-contained system of tracks. Because, like some raptor — an eagle, perhaps a double-eagle — looking for prey, then suddenly plunging down from the extreme heights of a retired bureaucrat's ether-blue concept-heaven upon our Julius Zihal (who was considering the prevailing conditions for observation at that point) came a tax office organizational guideline, which immediately, during that immeasurably short but decisive moment, became wedded to the newly presented and rather unusual material, from which arose that chemical union, that new dimension, that higher order or unio mystica (who cares, because basically such things are just trivialities!) which will make our report seem plausible.

The bureaucrat tried to orient himself very soon after entering his darkened bedroom. Not in the room itself, of course — there, without any sense of orientation, he bumped his hip rather liberally against the bedstead — but in the cosmic space outside, as it were, in the space of that new world of possibilities that had opened up to him. There things twinkled far and near, brightly and dimly, quietly giving off a gleam that was yellow, but in one case rose-colored, almost like the forest nymph — and enticing for that very reason. Yet, even more important: when the bureaucrat had passed through the dark doorway and his firmament of earthly stars had calmly and mysteriously presented itself to him and had become visible to him in its silent splendor — well, just briefly there had been something else and now it struck him, rather vaguely, of course, that it had been just that way with that first, surprising, penetrating gaze — that there had been something else which touched him just very gently, the way the thready breezes of Indian summer caress one's face; it was beautiful to stand there in the dark and look so deeply within and so far out beyond, it was beautiful even without . . . objects. And at the moment when the bureaucrat found that last word, he roared through the next switch, the third one, which was mentioned just a bit ago and which we consider the final and most decisive one, and distanced himself from his own amazed feeling with the great haste and never recalled afterward that he had just thought that incomprehensible fragment of an uncompleted sentence (and for him probably uncompletable as well) that went, ". . . one might actually be able to occupy oneself in a completely different way . . ."

Yes, whether the view is narrow or broad, it's always the same lights that appear in the evenings, in silent configurations, dim or sharp, or in gleaming repose. It's everyman's earthly, star-filled heaven, full of sickly, earth-bound stars that blink and twinkle just like those in the sky — and differently to the many, lonely pairs of eyes in those many windows and, most assuredly, precisely suited to each one. Whoever walks to the window, as our bureaucrat did there, walks beneath his constellation; and certainly even this glinting and distant greeting could be interpreted, if we were only able to do so.

With the word "ob-ject," however, the switch was thrown, forcefully and decisively, perhaps because that word "ob-ject" somehow had a tax-office tinge to it or was inwardly filled with its substance and hence had some magical effect for Juilius Zihal in that regard. Which, just for the brief, passing caress of an Indian summer's breeze — in that immeasurably brief pause when one part of the tax-office order-cosmos took over from another — was a world become free and formable as if by the touch of a magic wand and now transferred to a new system of coordinates.

The bureaucrat looked, first of all, to see what was closer and what was farther away, what was beaming in that heaven like a fixed star of the first magnitude — such as the "Forest Nymph" — and what was farther back and dim; then what lay to the right and left and what lay in the middle, directly opposite, or was situated unfavorably, lighted obliquely; and beyond that, what was above, what hung too high? Nothing, almost nothing, because the bureaucrat himself was located quite high in the sky, and so there were no cosmic sour grapes there. And finally: what lay lower, quite favorably in part, but sometimes just too far below, unless, of course, you could lower your eyes like plumb-bobs and direct them at a window, turned at right angles (like a periscope), eyeballs on long, vein-covered stalks, right outside someone's window, and scare to death anyone who might happen to look out . . . no, the bureaucrat wasn't prey to that sort of fantasy. Since the third switch he'd really become all too reasonable, the Double Eagle had ruffled his feathers, was playing a strange game with him. The three dimensions held fast, the interstellar space that had just been formed from chaos still trembled slightly.

But what did those stars portend? Some of them — bright, beaming, and obvious, stood far off in space — oh! Zihal would love to have been closer to them, and longing stirred in his heart. Others gleamed totally unconcealed at not too great a distance. The tall building opposite fell away at that point; one could look out freely over the lower part of the roof. Yes, those windows there, at about the same level . . . they had no curtains at all to speak of, but of course were farther away than the astonishing sight just seen from the adjoining room . . . well, the nonchalant attitude of those people in that regard was understandable; they probably thought there was no building facing them at all. Suddenly it occurred to Zihal that the apartment which he now occupied had not been rented for a rather long time before he moved in. Yes indeed, nonchalance was prevalent there and, if he remembered rightly, the concierge, on receiving the gratuity that was charged against the third part of the moving expenses, had remarked casually that the tenant prior to Zihal had been an old woman; so it was clearly a matter of not making anyone aware of the change there or of his own person. "Darkness helps" was what the bureaucrat thought, literally. And then came the half-muffled echo from the depths of his soul: "And opera glasses would, too, or some such thing . . ." At the very same moment, those windows on the same level across the way showed signs of life. And what life! A cozy one. He shook every which way as the spirit of the hunt came over him; it was as if he were immersed to his neck in rapidly bubbling soda water. Now he was hurrying back to the rear window. To the right, below, where his building protruded forward, with a view from almost directly above — what was that?! Meanwhile, light sprang back from one of the windows directly opposite. Pouff! Completely dark. And only now — out of the corner of his eye, that half-sensation was now becoming definite, and now it whirled him around! — did the bureaucrat realize that the goddess herself had appeared in the constellation "Forest Nymph." His breath failed him, his heart almost ceased its activity (and he banged his hip against the bedstead — those were the circumstances under which that happened). And then — even that star burned out, leaped back into interstellar darkness, and another one here and there another one — swallowed up, gone. The bureaucrat sat down on his bed exhausted, his heart pounding; then finally he took off his clothes slowly in the dark and crept in between the covers.

7

The next day was overcast, at first shot through by isolated arrows of sunlight which here and there cut into the gloom that had gathered and caused it to be critically visible, so to speak. From the kitchen came the hoarse, grumbling noise of the coffee grinder, muffled by the intervening walls. The bureaucrat was sleeping. When his housekeeper entered the bedroom there ensued a confused and mostly improvised awakening on the part of Zihal, much like what happens when someone suddenly attacks a piano with splayed, untutored fingers. He avoided the Zadichekian gaze. Besides, it was a breach of decorum that he was still lying there and only his attempt to restore that decorum prevented the bureaucrat from cutting himself with his razor during the hasty toilette which began after the Zadichek woman had slipped back into the department where she was in charge, namely, the kitchen. But that act of shaving soon brought back a proper attitude and relaxed execution, leaving no room for haste, errors, and improprieties.

The bureaucrat proceeded to the kitchen to have his coffee. On his way, he picked up a pencil and several of the saved pages of the grocer's wall calendar (even this part of the inventory had been moved and now found itself in its proper place, a detail which Frau Zadichek had taken care of automatically, as belonging within her own sphere of influence). In the kitchen, the announcement was made to Frau Zadichek that henceforth and until further notice the evening meal would not be taken at home and that accordingly she need not be concerned with preparing anything. (We concur in that arrangement, find it reasonable and understandable and will keep focused on the fact that you have to be able to see what you're eating in order to enjoy the meal — to stuff something into yourself in the dark strikes us, as it did the bureaucrat as well, as being undignified.) During breakfast — in other words, relaxed and comfortable — the bureaucrat jotted down the following preliminary observations and guidelines on the paper: "Directly opposite, Window I, 10 o'clock, to be considered 'impressive'; Window II, opposite, circa 10:10 — 'very impressive'; Window III, view downward and to the right, 10:15, q.i. ('quite impressive'); Window II, Forest Nymph, 'most impressive,' sets standard for highest category, nearly simultaneously w/ W.III. According to preliminary observations."

However, that morning he went on to read, apparently with undiminished attention, the following regulations in the Handbook of Administrative Practices:

Quarterly payment of Salary and Living Allowance

To all subsidiary departments:

With reference to §48, para. 2 and §169 para. 2 of the law of 25 January 19..Gov't. Bull. Nr. 15 (HAP) and to the Central Ministry Directive of 1 February 19.., Govt. Bull. Nr. 33 (Adm.Bull. Nr. 31), your attention is directed to the following:

By 30 April, 19.. at the latest, each official (Civil Servant) is to make written declaration as to whether payment of his salary shall be made monthly or quarter-yearly on the officially determined dates. Furthermore, this declaration is only admissible in cases of initial assignment, transfer to a different service location, as well as promotion to a higher salary level and in cases of marriage or the termination of marriage . . .

(Zihal had not taken advantage of this during his term of service and that was gratifying to him, even if it occasioned a melancholy, sidelong glance.)

. . . and is to be handed in within thirty days after the respective event . Should no declaration be submitted, it will be assumed, in the case of initial assignment, that the official (Civil Servant) elects a quarterly payment of salary, and that in all other cases, no alteration of the prevailing payment schedule is desired. Declarations submitted late will not be considered.

The declaration is to be directed to the departmental office, does not require the affixation of a special stamp, and is to be submitted for processing without delay.

The payment of salary shall begin on the next officially determined date, provided the declaration has been properly executed and submitted prior to the first day of the month in which the payment date falls.

In the case of salaries paid on a quarterly basis, the appropriate receipt stamp fee is to be deducted from the payment; at that time, separate receipts should be provided for other reimbursements and allowances.

> Should an official (Civil Servant) whose salary is being
> paid on a quarterly basis become entitled to a higher
> salary during a given quarter, then this will be taken
> into account at the next payment of his wages, by
> arranging in each case for restitution to be made in
> monthly installments equivalent to the *excess* salary
> accumulated.

The last sentence had a depressive effect. The word "excess" was
quite capable of insinuating itself into private life as well, like a
tiny stone that can be felt in one's shoe under certain circumstances.

8

In the afternoon, the weather cleared up completely. Zihal
picked up his hat and coat — the brisk movement with which he
stuck his hand into the sleeve had something of a decision about it,
or actually was one. The part of the city to which the bureaucrat
took himself can be considered as office-divorced, as totally
office-foreign, by virtue of its style, its atmosphere — that's clear;
not to say, however, that the organs and tentacles of the tax office
would not have felt their way in there in certain cases, if need be
— and was there anywhere they hadn't felt around by now? No,
every human being was subject to assessment in some form, is
subject to it, will always be subject to it. But only when the office
has outlived human beings, when organic life on this planet has
long since died out, but still remains susceptible of assessment (at
least for insufficient precision in filling out forms) by some office,
only then will the complete autonomy of the institution be
incontrovertible and not exposed to the degrading suspicion of
having some purpose or other — only then, when the last supports
fall away like scaffolding and the building is standing there alone,
indeed, with its very essence visible now for the first time, l'art
pour l'art, noble, having outlasted everything, formed and con-
figured down the the very last details of room 479C.

In the meantime (while we were digressing dithyrambically),

the part of that spirit that is standing right in front of us, Julius Zihal by name, had already covered a large part of his way — to the vicinity of that broad arm of the Danube which has been regulated into a canal that flows gray-green through the inner districts of Vienna, opening up an endlessly unfolding, curved stage setting of houses as well as larger structures that front on it, between which, here and there, bridges leap over its deeply sunken bed. There, with its towers reaching an almost oppressive height, rose a red brick building, that looked just like one of those toy forts for little boys, made to look just like a real fortress with bastions and battlements and loopholes; and the battlements are perhaps the most important thing. That view must have been shared by the architect of this red stronghold (below which, small but confident, a bureaucrat is walking by) as well, because he more than amply crowned all of the upper borders of his awful structure with such battlements — he stuck them on wherever even barely possible, even if, in truth, there was really nothing else playful about that ponderous monstrosity of a building, which, in fact, was designed with nothing of the sort in mind. Much to the contrary. The towers contained elevators for artillery pieces, which could be deployed up there on the mighty, battlement-crowned platforms to sweep a large section of the city. That's exactly what was intended in the days directly after the Revolution of 1848, when the authorities were still suffering from a sort of shock. Several such fortificatory monstrosities came into existence in Vienna at that time and, during the second half of the century, a plentiful supply of bugs marched into them from all sides, and, you could say say, to the tune of clinking blades. In addition, our red structure may have exerted its attraction on them by means of its related color, because in the time after the Great World War, when for many years in a row the barracks and the military were all but forgotten, a few companies of soldiers still had to be stationed there to provide the poor little creatures with the bare essentials of nourishment.

The bureaucrat continued his dignified progress around the rectangle, to whose spirit he may well have felt himself related in some remote way, although it can scarcely be presumed that this penetrated to his level of consciousness. But he was, of course, free from the disagreeable sensations that certain sorts of people (various authorities have a fine nose for sensing such things) experience while passing structures of that sort; and so he walked on happily beside the many red stones. Eventually it finally came to an end, as did the bureaucrat's path as well, for Herr Julius Zihal was at his destination.

The latter presented itself in a strange configuration, as a cross between Roman ruins — fortifications or aqueducts perhaps — and a termite hill, but without much height — flat, low, with dingy whitewash and countless arcades, between which, here and there, a crevice or passageway seemed to lead deep into the interior and, during the course of two paces, afforded the passerby a glance into a space oddly packed with household goods and appliances of every conceivable sort; and in some way or other it was as if one could look into his own body cavity and into his intestines, or into the lowest story of dawning consciousness, or into the storerooms of the past, where, astonishingly, absolutely everything is still preserved, right down to the smallest item, still standing there and taken seriously, like something from the same day that's still in one's hand or in front of one's eyes. But, actually, those halls and arcades were not just figuratively, but quite literally the storerooms of the past, where the abandoned inventory of many hundreds of lives had accumulated, articles that had been ejected from some unknown biography or other, coldly and heartlessly, although they may have been its faithful companions for a long, long time — trunks, tables, chairs, saddles, telescopes, watches, pistols, and riding boots — and all that was left for them now was the monotonous company of their own kind. Each of them had experienced the same disloyalty in some form or other and had ended up on that desolate pile, in those dirty, whitewashed, rectangular halls with arcades around them, the city's flea market, called the "Tandelmarkt" in Vienna. Everything there was "tand," or trumpery, because even the devotion with which this person or that may have clung almost fanatically to some object or possession, to some dear thing or other given by some dear hand, because even that devotion had turned out to be mere play-acting by the soul, mere trumpery — at least when things got tough. Or someone's heirs may have thrown out something that seemed useless to them — out into a foreign, disconnected world. There it lay now in some dark corner, looked at, or not, merely on the basis of the price being asked, deprived of the touch of its former master's hand which nourished its soul every time he picked it up from its shelf and inspected it lovingly. And now it exuded — increasingly feebly to be sure — the scent of its previous owner's life, banished there to that place of dust and junk, to that purgatory of things which tried to drive out their individuality, their past, and their sense of pride, to that prison of commercial compulsion which attempts to reduce everything to the same level, to that way-station for migratory souls — which, nevertheless and despite all its gloominess, occasionally released a piece — and often a quite unprepossessing one — to a new, and, now and then, splendid life, highly prized because of its value as an antique, which the previous owner hadn't appreciated. But no enduring soul can be picked up by such a commercial handle. That plump, little, rococo Venus, for example, created in 1771 by the Viennese ceramicist Melchior, an absolutely dear and even modest appearing lady — although she's dropped her red cloak so that no further concealment offends the eye, with the exception of her tiny right hand which absolutely belongs just where it is, all the while looking so gently and shamefully — that tiny Venus, for example, had moved into the palace of a count after not too long a stay at the way-station for migratory souls, because Count Mucki Langingen used to like to poke around there at the Tandelmarkt and so that's where he'd come across the tiny, naked lady, instead of at some antique store where she really belonged. There's a quite obvious connection with Zihal when I mention here that for years the father of that young count occupied the highest part of that ethereally blue concept heaven — from the bureaucrat's viewpoint anyway — because he'd been the Minister of Finance. From there were handed down all those revisions of the Handbook of Adminis-trative Practices which were subsequently put into effect by the various departments.

The Venus had been standing on one of the shelves of a buffet that occupied a spot deep within one of those crevice-like passageways, totally surrounded by other pieces of furniture, some piled on top of each other, some displaying nothing more than their unfinished backsides to the onlooker; but among all those pieces there amidst the gloom, the chill, and the smell of long-settled dust, so completely foreign to the usual whirl of outside life — among all those pieces there were passageways through which one could approach them from a different side, so that they could be looked at from that perspective as well. And if one looked more closely, it would become apparent that the entire, seemingly random arrangement had been carried out extremely cleverly, so that everything in that labyrinth, where life had been spun into a cocoon, could be reached (in other words, things there were basically just like they are in our memories and in the storerooms of the past in our own innards). Even the projecting shelf of that oak buffet remained accessible to Count Mucki. Many old glasses were resting there in their cool dust, two of them extremely beautiful and valuable, but mixed in among things that belonged in a kitchen. The young Count took the glasses. Behind lay several other items all pushed together, leather cases and who knows what all, and then there was Venus, standing there trying to conceal her shame as best she could when she was caught in the act.

Now she was standing, enchanting and worthy of admiration as she was, in the vitrine of the Dowager Countess, in a room whose pale light may have been due to the fact that the predominant violets and whites there collided in a not particularly tasteful way, while luckily the blue of the sky and the foamy gray-green of the crowns of the trees in the park remained somewhat less prominent, because the room had a projecting balcony and the trees stood far back, where the sky touched a small, white, stone pavilion at the edge of one's field of vision, changing slowly and monotonously off in the distance the way things do in so-called nature. The tiny goddess, who of course was possessed of a enduring soul in keeping with her status, was not particularly impressed with the entourage here — suitable at least, but at the same time rather mediocre. She had known other surroundings, which, even if more modest by worldly standards, constantly "hovered in front of her" as the ones actually suited to her status — which could be taken literally, because she seemed to be standing in the air, hovering back there to the right of the stone pavilion, whose round dome glowed on its near side in the late afternoon sun; it was as if she were there spatially, or perhaps just a bit behind it, but not behind in the flow of time. Carried far and wide in it, fully fifty or a hundred years — who knows how many? — like a ship of clouds sailing in the distance, drifted the poet's room, in which the goddess had dwelled together with her owner, standing in a small console above his bed, her tiny hand covering a hundred years ago what it still covered today, and in her head memories cast in translucent porcelain. Well, back then she had, of course, realized that she was in the proper place, where — below her on the bed, beside her on the table — night and day, often in the extremes of desperation, there was a constant struggle for lines that were obviously not to be seen with the physical eye, that had no connection with external happiness and prosperity, and no relationship at all to personal life — because the latter went on uniformly and unaltered like a clock with three or four figures of friends who walked out at their appointed hours, then disappeared back into the housing. But the enduring soul of porcelain really knew what was going on there; it seemed noble to her and it seemed proper to her, and when all fell quiet and the pen ran lightly across the paper and the sunbeams poured in through the window and spread throughout the room the glow of the bright curtains in which was contained all the animation and the open squares and the fruit markets dripping with color, which were all part of that so southerly city, why, then, soon nearly everything was contained in that room and it was impossible to be cut off and closed in, for the simple reason that that small room was able to swallow in the big world, bit by bit — well, now, at such times, the tiny lady in the console above the narrow divan was not at all haughty and nothing appeared mediocre to her, as it did here in the Dowager Countess' room, where, at best, she could do the art-historical honors; but there, in the room of her now long-dead friend and owner, it seemed natural and fitting to add her modest note to an already well-rounded chord, to stand there in the console and let the nakedness of her body shimmer in the late afternoon sunlight in which lay the orange-colored glow of the slightly moving curtain, the call of the peddler echoing from the distance punctuated by the trot of a horse that was being ridden by somewhere, and always to the accompaniment of the brittle, whispering voice of the pen.

The author whom she watched while he was writing on such occasions — a Frenchman or an Italian — had very large, dark eyes; and, having settled on the eyes, time cast in porcelain suddenly began to move, to swirl rapidly, go shooting off darkly, and it eventually rushed and splashed like a huge mass of water against the way station for migratory souls — those, that is, who can be deprived of their souls — right into that fantastic passageway or crevice where the oak buffet was standing and right up there next to her erstwhile neighbor on the shelf. And now similar eyes were looking at her there, that is, similar to those of the poet in a certain sense. These eyes were big, and actually made everything they looked at seem larger and more distinct; they were deep, like passageways or tunnels leading away to the rear, and they would have been — if a fine layer of cool, old dust hadn't mellowed them and made them more kindly and forbearing — rather blazing. As it was, however, despite their strongly protruding curvature, they looked more like the eyes of a nice, old gentleman; they were gazing directly at the little rococo Venus (and the latter would perhaps have been ashamed if that gaze had fallen upon her gleaming and undiminished), and they were looking out from a leather case whose lid, lined with blue silk, was standing open. They were the eyes of an old pair of field glasses.

They had seen a lot. Actually, it was as if they belonged to an old courtier and his good manners had such a forthright character. For instance, he occasionally remarked to the tiny goddess that, despite the fact that he was so close to her, he would very much like to see her even more clearly by turning the focusing screw, if he were only able to do it himself. That's how enchanting she was!

He'd seen a great deal — even something that would have been simply unimaginable to the retired bureaucrat Julius Zihal, namely, the Double Eagle with its feathers ruffled. Yes, indeed, the latter was to be seen in that state at Königgrätz in the year 1866, ruffled by the Prussians and seen by that old courtier with the glass eyes. And for that reason we're going to call him the "Sixty-Sixer." There are certain reasons for assuming — not really definite reasons, just assumptions — for assuming, anyway, that the Double Eagle had never quite forgotten those field glasses, most certainly not, considering that they'd had been there on the Austrian side as a witness to the malheur . . . and hence one could conceive that a tiny little bit of the Double Eagle's resentment had been directed toward those field glasses from that day on, a resentment that lusted to do some ruffling.

But not to the Prussians, because they'd long since been totally ruffled for good. Those nice, old-fashioned field glasses were almost like an instrument of fate, as will perhaps be noticed later.

The old Sixty-Sixer had little hope of getting away from there in the near future, a fact for which the great progress made in the optical industry since his years of active duty no doubt bore much of the blame. Since the departure of the tiny goddess he was even starting to become somewhat lethargic, because nothing caught his eye or excited his attention any more, and besides that, his gaze was gradually beginning to cloud over more than just a little because of the layer of dust that had settled on him. He began to drift off. One could say that he reflected inwardly; there was something going on within him that was like a prolonged, extended sunset, namely the sunset of what he seriously considered to be the ultimate, introspective evening of his life, because he didn't believe in the migration of souls (and that was, at least in his case, a mistake). The sunset which he took to be his own was, however, that of a so-called epoch or era, or that of an eon — designations noteworthy for the fact that there is something about all of them that is like a vague, blurred image of a sort of last judgment painted on the wall of a lunatic's cell — anyway, it was something of that sort and thus the inwardly reflected sunset of the Sixty -Sixer also contained images that, in and of themselves, belong to the light of day: silhouetted cleanly against the sky, there are hills or modest elevations, from the crests of which something is coming down toward us everywhere, simultaneous with the dying away of the cannon fire that had crowned them, along with individual, rounded puffs of smoke that are dissolving now, becoming less frequent, no longer replacing one another, because all the batteries are pulling back. Here they come now, down the shallow incline at a trot, a few at the gallop; now one can hear the rattling, can see the cannoneers bouncing on their caissons, holding on with both hands. But one of the batteries is missing and off to the left where the hills rise up a little and some of the underbrush stands out against the sky — indeed, one might even be able to see grass on the nearer ridge, but, of course, that would only be possible with the Sixty-Sixer — off to the left, out of sight, one battery is firing incessantly, as if it were complaining loudly and angrily about the retreat of the others. Actually, no one paid much attention to it at the time, but later that battery became famous, and more recently even found its way into world history as an anecdote, something which, by the way, can happen to anyone and a lot more easily than is generally and solemnly believed, hence a word to the wise: the situation doesn't always have to be as worthy of admiration as it was for that artillery battery. How would we look if we were suddenly immortalized in our usual state of affairs, in other words, during those weak moments that last for hours?

9

You know the whole story already: the bureaucrat's going to buy that Sixty-Sixer. . . well, you didn't quite know everything, because he's already bought it during the time made available by our long digression. Coming around the corner from the brick building with the battlements, he circled the square filled with antiques and looked into its caverns and into its crevices and passageways and between mirrors, bedsteads, boots, alabaster lamps and saddles and then on into the enteric confusion of his own inner self (he didn't know that, of course) where those crumbling and fissured little walls had been built up from rubble piled on top of more rubble, which end up separating a person from his own past just as well as any mountain. From within those crevices, emerging from between piles of junk, feeling their way around old chests, becoming visible between articles of clothing and hanging saddlery, the dealers soon made their way into the light, having smelled a customer in that respectable appearing gentlemen who had walked by several times and looked more like a buyer than a seller. "An' what would the gentleman like t' have . . . ?" they called out here and there. Had the souls of dead bugs from the neighboring red fortress migrated into human bodies? It certainly looked that way.

Don't go thinking that the bureaucrat was taken advantage of. Impossible. The distance between him and the dealers was so gigantic, like the span of a great weight-bearing arch in that ordered world within him, that he totally anticipated being taken advantage of, not at all in the usual form of casual mistrust but, rather, in a completely human, indeed, benevolent way: he totally granted those dealers the right to try to cheat him in advance, much the same way he granted himself the bureaucratic characteristics of those bygone days.

He hung it around his neck, the Sixty-Sixer, in its case, on a strap, in such a way that it adorned his bureaucrat's neck quite strategically. The vendor had had a piece of soft chamois leather on hand and cleaned the dust off the lenses. They now had a deep, blank stare, dark as night. Julius turned his steps away from the precincts of the second-hand dealers. The object on his breast now assured him unambiguously of a new phase in his life. This had now become something that would remain in force, which had an existence beyond his own person, beyond the presence or absence of the latter, indifferent to inclinations or disinclinations — that's just the objective character, the character of all so-called affairs or whatever you might call the serious aspects of life (because basically such things are just trivialities). The bureaucrat headed toward the arm of the Danube. It can't be denied that he felt burdened somehow; indeed, for a few moments his sense of his own life was somewhat like that of a fly that knows it's finally about to be caught by the swatter. Added to that was the fact that the object in question was not going to sit still, but was displaying movement of its own, as it were: now it was going to be necessary to buy an electric flashlight, something small and handy that threw a concentrated beam of light like a louvered lantern. Yes, and now he was going to need a lamp with a shade for his own apartment as well! But right now he wanted to look through the field glasses, along the canal; of course he'd tried them out carefully at the second-hand dealer's, before finalizing the sale (by looking at the ornaments along the roof lines of buildings and at distant windows). But to look across the water, at a greater distance — that was tempting — a sort of gratuity added to the practical side of things. He entered the park along the riverbank, with its promenade — one of those localities where time seems to pass more slowly and almost seems to stand still for decades, despite all the great changes elsewhere, because the spring sun on baby carriages, gossiping mothers, women with packages, laborers sitting and chewing on their sandwiches, and finally the little boys and girls running back and forth, with their echoing voices, because all of those completely unchanging appearances are, as it were, the lingering undertones of life — and so Zihal entered the river bank park and was soon given a nickname by the boys playing there: "The Admiral." Not bad. Because the bureaucrat had put his left hand on the railing on the wall along the quay while holding the glasses in his right hand and looking out over the water and along the canal to a bridge where several big barges were tied up. The children waited behind Herr Zihal to see what was going to happen next, and he sensed that; and even a few scattered adults looked over from their benches. Indeed, two people stopped walking and looked in the direction indicated by the Sixty-Sixer. There the pale, gray-green arc of water extended off to the left from beneath a bridge, on which the pedestrians and vehicles looked like beetles creeping along a pole. The buildings on the opposite side of the canal were stacked up in a long line, unequal in height, like stairs, while the already variably bright green trees that bordered the scene all seemed to have been drawn along in the direction of the water, arranging themselves into a broader river that flowed, on both sides of the narrower one, deeper into the distance that opened up, into the opening that had been forced into the sea of houses.

The old spyglasses were good, even if the degree of magnification of the objects they brought closer to the bureaucrat was just a modest one. The Admiral shoved the glasses back into their case. He was experiencing — perhaps for the first time in his life — a sort of feeling of being thrown back upon himself — in other words, unfortunately, on a person with whom he had no idea what to do (because basically such things are just trivialities). The field glasses exerted a slight pressure as they lay just above his abdomen. Zihal had left the riverbank park. He wandered through those office-foreign streets, surrounded by pale light, struck by new associations, ready for previously unheard-of deeds.

Of which the first was the purchase of a small electric pocket flashlight in a store that sold such things, whose sign had soon appeared, had almost popped up out of the bureaucrat himself, so that he didn't have to spend much time looking around for it. He walked out into the street again, with the bells on the door carrying on their shrill jingling behind him, the small object tucked away in his pocket as if it were part of the field glasses on his breast. And Julius Zihal, taken as a whole, now felt himself inside of a sort of tough but completely transparent wrapper that separated him from the rest of the world, that set him beside it in a way — if one is permitted to say such a thing. You frequently see that sort of colorless, transparent material used in stores where sweets are sold, to make wrappers or little sacks to pack things up with. The bureaucrat himself was walking in a sack, as it were, in the sack of his own condition, of his own self-consciousness; but inside that closed universe, however, two bodies revolved in their own orbits, namely the field glasses and the pocket flashlight. The fixed constellation of the Forest Nymph, with its pinkish glow, remained aloof, yet perceptible, out there.

For that reason, if we now set our bureaucrat down in some café completely unfamiliar to him, he'll present a remarkably different picture from the one we'd expect to find within a frame labeled "A Bureaucrat in the Coffee House," where he'd receive the appropriate greeting from the "marqueur," and be served "the usual," where he'd inspect the periodicals, then read the daily news, using the text as well as the pictures to provide the basis for his next crystalline presentation at the Stammtisch; where he'd smoke, clear his throat, completely at ease; but but we would certainly not expect to see him tied up in a little, transparent sack with field glasses on his chest and a flashlight in his pocket . . . but even that wouldn't be the most decisive difference. Be that as it may, however, what happened was that the bureaucrat, in his muted or restrained or isolated condition, asked himself what he was really doing there in that out-of-the-way and relatively untidy café. He remained seated in his sack without finding out. He paged through the newspapers and periodicals. But as far as really examining them was concerned — a critical, analytical act, if you will — solid ground for that was totally missing inside his sack. Zihal, gazing out of the window, thought he saw things that somehow seemed inappropriate, even offensive: a young boy was standing on the corner across the street, sucking on something, when suddenly a disheveled woman appeared, slapped the boy in the face and dragged him off around the corner. Right after that a fancy automobile drove by slowly, with a chauffeur and a servant up front and three boisterously laughing, elegant women in the back seat, which left Julius Zihal with the sensation that the door to a greenhouse filled with strong-smelling flowers — hyacinths perhaps — had been torn open and then slammed shut again. In front of the café door — right there in front of him, on the edge of the sidewalk by the lamp post — a dog lifted his right hind leg in a way familiar to everyone.

Now that was going too far for the bureaucrat and in order to preserve his critical dignity, he now took the silver watch out of his vest pocket — only, however, to establish an irrefutable fact which immediately did away with that dignity and inner repose and plunged him into the river of extreme haste: it was nearly ten minutes to six. It was only now that he noticed that it was starting to get dark. At that moment a third body with its own circular orbit around his universe suddenly came into being with a pop: called . . . the note pad. Because the grocer's calendar was fastened to the wall and was totally unsuitable for writing down, by the narrow beam of a flashlight, astronomical data such as the rise of certain constellations above the horizon line. This required some convenient writing surface which at the same time offered firm support. The bureaucrat paid and stumbled over the doorstep of the café. There on that street not a paper store was to be seen. He hurried around the corner into the next one and thought he saw what he was looking for. But the shutters had already been pulled down. However, diagonally across the street from him beckoned a green glass sign with white lettering which said "Paper." Taking a chance, Zihal raced across on an angle; a piercing, screeching noise became audible — the brakes of an automobile behind him — compared to which the crude words of the driver sounded soft and fuzzy. When the bureaucrat finally left the paper store, the sought-after writing pad clamped under his arm, he stopped on the sidewalk and looked up and down the street, only now, after the fact, paying any attention to the place and the surroundings where he'd been involved in this almost panic-stricken incident.

10

Problems are presented by the following, namely, the subsequent Zihalian evenings and nights — with respect to the choice of modes of description, that is. If one were tempted, for example, in view of the erratic and totally sporadic nature of the events, to assume a tone that is the absolute opposite, perhaps one that is as solid as iron, in order to allow all that absurd creeping and milling around to stand out more clearly against the background of such an attitude: "Julius, omnibus hic pertinentibus rebus bene gestis, et postquam iam dudum coenam apud cauponem commederat, habitatione sua intrata eam illuminare faustum not putavit." When a ringing tone is called for, the language of the Romans is always the best one. In German, the whole sentence reads, "he didn't want to turn the light on."

He managed to bang against the edges of the tables, especially in the kitchen, but the transparent sack — tied closed at the top — in which the bureaucrat was hidden, resisted with its elasticity; luckily the collision did not involve the new flashlight. Window 0 (kitchen) was left out of the "concept" after short deliberation. There'd be time enough. He had to find the pencil, but without allowing any light to show — which seemed ill-advised because of Window I (directly opposite, to be considered as "impressive," 10 o'clock). We mentioned earlier that married men, on returning home in the evening, customarily send their long asses' ears ahead on reconnaissance. However, even the bureaucrat, despite being a bachelor — or actually, a widower — now came sneaking into his own dwelling, his antennas feeling ahead in the dark, then stole from room to room, letting his louvered lantern shine into the corners.

There was something mysterious about it, something like a solemn prelude, as he went about in the dark, opening all three windows of his apartment — the entry portals for the images from his new, star-filled sky. The net had been stretched, the lurking spider sat within it, tiny eyes taking in ad notam whatever might be happening (and actually, the writing tablet, pencil, and small flashlight were lying ready at hand!), the Sixty-Sixer, inhabited by the resentful soul of the double eagle, sent out his flashing, probing gaze. And it did happen! The laws of astronomy really held true even in this new system of spatial coordinates: directly opposite, Window I, 10 o'clock, "to be considered as impressive" — light sprang punctually into the rectangle. "Take aim!" seemed to come from the Sixty-Sixer, like a military command from the old days when people standing in orderly rows shot at each other. This was the first great shock: scarcely had the screw been turned when the bureaucrat already found himself, so to speak, across the way, in the blond woman's room, standing scarcely three steps away from her.

What took place — what he saw, in other words — was

identical to what had happened the last time and yet it moved the bureaucrat more forcefully than anything he'd been able to see or imagine back then. The lenses trembled. Here was the leap onto the new Zihalian tracks, the creative point which, overtaken to be sure and repeated the same evening in completely different degrees of clarity and astonishment, nevertheless remained stronger in its aftereffects and penetrated more deeply than anything that happened afterward. Here, standing open again, was the crevice from which the numbing vapors had spilled forth, wrapping the bureaucrat in deep confusion — indeed in a new life form — tighter and tighter to the point of complete closure, tying up that little sack in which he was now contained.

The light was extinguished across the way; the rectangle of the window stood black and mute. Zihal drew back. At the far side of the room he squatted down again. The small flashlight sent its beam at his pocket watch: 10:07. Everything checked out: directly opposite, Window I, "to be considered as impressive." Actually, very impressive indeed — but in view of the individual bits of data presenting themselves, that comparatively higher classification had been reserved for the some of the cases already investigated. On the page from the grocer's calendar where the latter had been noted — listed in chronological order which, incidentally, coincided with the ranking according to relative qualifications, from lowest to highest — Zihal made a check mark next to the first note.

The orderly and, one might almost say, dignified bearing of the aforementioned small proceedings ruled out any sort of haste — nonetheless, the next observation was scheduled for 10:10, Window II, opposite, "very impressive." He managed to feel his way into the next room in the dark and even from the door he could see the object in question brightly illuminated, far more brightly than before. Here, for the first time, certain lightning-fast processes that combined thought and imagination appeared within the bureaucrat and accompanied him constantly from then on in his strange preoccupation, like a cloud of mosquitoes whose swarming and buzzing drove him on — and, to put it clearly, deeper and deeper into a striving for absolute completeness and the best possible utilization of every opportunity: nothing could be allowed to escape him. It was a striving for totality. The best site for observation had to be chosen, the optimal arrangements made from the optical standpoint, and not a second missed. Scarcely had Zihal caught sight of the three bright, not very distant windows — in the silence, they seemed to line up and come right into his dark room there with their bright light, meaningfully, as if those apartments were pushing themselves together every night in a dream, without anyone's having noticed; inside and outside became totally mixed up. Anyway, scarcely had the bureaucrat caught sight of the majestic object when he thought, "I've been missing something over there — they've turned off the really bright light, now perhaps there's going to be something more . . . " He was standing at "Window, Roman Numeral Two" and took aim. His fingers flew to the focusing screw, at the same time he repositioned himself farther to the left with mincing little steps, thus improving the viewing conditions. Those conditions, strived for, prepared for, and, so far as possible, kept on a refined level, now came over him, came down on his head, struck him; he was put in the position of the man "who doesn't quite know what to make of a good thing," he was like a shallow saucer that's held under the stream of a fountain and which — remains empty. A cataract can't be caught with a thimble.

In the room off to the left with obviously only a single window, a buxom, young, black-haired woman was leisurely washing herself from top to bottom, exposing to the bureaucrat and the dark-eyed gaze of the Sixty-Sixer the various landscapes of her imposing body: hill, mountain, and valley, all soaped and gleaming statuesquely. But Zihal, who harbored a certain quiet, moustache-stroking preference for slightly more mature female types, managed — not just for that reason, but for the totality of the situation — to recover from the blow after the passage of just a little time. The Sixty-Sixer now stabbed as deeply as possible into the two-windowed room off to the right. And what it spitted over there and brought back . . . but at that moment the bright light was turned off and remained burning only in the window to the left.

Shocked, indeed devastated and full of grief, the bureaucrat once again sought inner equanimity and raison d'être in the earlier, gleaming, soapy manifestation. And soon satisfied and reaffirmed to a considerable degree, he then went on to discover, by means of a slight adjustment in the direction of the glasses, that the level of illumination over on the other side had not fallen away to nothing, was not completely unfavorable; as far as the viewing conditions were concerned (the viewing site could be improved still further by a gradual move over to the right side of the window sill), they could be considered quite favorable because of moderate, but nonetheless distinct — contoured and gently distinct, as it were, indeed quite inviting — illumination from the side, from the head end of the double bed where obviously there were small floor lamps. Indeed, here everything could probably be grouped under one heading, with those venerable parents and their charming girl (the latter was making use of the towel at that point); however, the barb of his obsession with completeness, with totality, the suction-like force of uncompleted tasks tore the bureaucrat away — regardless of whether his subtle arrangements had already fulfilled their purpose in as ideal a way as possible — from that feast for the eyes. And besides: if the proverb "variatio delectat" (change delights) is going to be valid anywhere, it's here — well, of course, not an all-encompassing validity, because that sentence certainly doesn't describe the case of Herr Julius Zihal completely, it only illuminates it from a certain direction; otherwise the case would turn out to be a much more casual, inconsequential one, a sort of high-level trumpery, but certainly not the dim and mute process of humanization, in other words, the development of a person in its very incipient stages.

He slipped away from the window, squatted down, turned his flashlight on the page from the grocer's wall catalog and wrote, "Window II, directly opposite: advance time to 10 o'clock." But then he deserted that post. Haste was necessary! Window III, view downward and to the right, 10:15! (quite impressive). Careful there! The row of four dark windows just above was quite close, at his level, belonged to his own building which projected around a sort of half-courtyard. The draft of a notice went gliding through the bureaucrat's mind as he slowly approached the left side of the window sill in the dark: "Window III to be considered less suitable because of possibility of counter-observation." But what splendid viewing conditions, contrary to expectation, actually, and what a favorable degree of illumination! Two objects. Nothing to stroke one's moustache over. Just the opposite. But there was a certain catch to the situation: the bureaucrat was unable to watch the two young girls between the ages of sixteen and eighteen without being a little bit moved. The one had her feet in a wash basin filled with water. The dear children! The two of them walked back and forth in the room (in fact, the display continually gained in freshness, provided surprises — in short, achieved the highest level of impressiveness), remaining totally hidden here and there for the tiniest little while, all of which resulted in the bureaucrat's constantly shuffling back and forth, changing his position in order to improve the viewing conditions so that nothing would be missed — and this led to recurring nervous tension and turmoil. Zihal was already beginning to feel the stress of this new activity of his, of the entire new area of responsibility. Added to that was the steady pressure of concern that emanated from the dark row of windows across the way, like a dark board against his forehead. The glasses frequently went swivelling over to inspect the black rectangles which loomed up mutely. One casement window, directly opposite, stood open. Zihal was already feeling displeasure. Was that sort of disturbance really necessary? According to protocol and for the sake of completeness, the Sixty-Sixer sent its parallel-chambered gaze to the left as well, into the open field of vision, at which point Zihal had to lean out of the window a little bit. ("Inspection of field to left of Window III with absolute minimum of forward lean because of possible counter-observation.") During the current time frame, the glasses pulled in only dark masses that fled in clumps through the moving field of vision — roofs, bare fire — walls, rows of light-dead windows, their outer surfaces catching the beams of the street lights, gables and roof borders rising up in the night, sooty and dim. He obtained a kind of relief through the realization that "for the moment there is nothing to be accomplished on this side." There was plenty of work as it was! He moved back slowly and carefully, crouched down behind the foot of the bed, and made the proper notation on the grocer's wall calendar for each of the events just monitored. Now it was time to retrace his steps and concentrate completely on Window II. As he straightened up, the bureaucrat edged forward slightly and took one more glance at the "view downward and to the right." Without a doubt, still to be considered very impressive! But weren't those children ever going to get done with their evening toilette?

Suddenly, however, it appeared to the bureaucrat that the previously open casement window in the darkness directly across from him was now closed.

He remained standing, motionless, then slowly and calmly allowed the Sixty-Sixer to rise — an admiral on the alert, who's been scanning the horizon for enemy frigates, and has just caught sight of them. But it could have been an illusion, light reflected in some way that made the window look open. Zihal stood as motionless as if he were cast iron. But over there, too, everything remained rigid and immobile in the mute darkness, in that state of neglect reserved for all of those things that do indeed belong to human habitation but never have any attention paid to them because they're hardly ever seen: the undersurfaces of tables, the tops of door frames and such. Everything completely legitimate, but dark. Even the train whistle which now sounded, distant and prolonged, was a legitimate, orderly voice. At that moment, Zihal felt strangely isolated from the world. He felt, so to speak, that he was stuck in a closed sack, that he was standing beside life — the way a door must feel when it's been taken off it hinges and is leaning against the wall. In complete silence, that dark room had carried itself, together with the bureaucrat, far away from anything that had to do with a bureaucrat or the Double Eagle.

But the latter, hiding in the Sixty-Sixer like the genie in the bottle, jumped out and ruffled his feathers admonishingly. Zihal turned around. Just a cursory glance to check the situation — out of a sense of duty, the way an engineer takes a quick look at the position of a lever — flitted across the impressive bits opposite Window II. However, the trills of alternating current had already been cut off from the situation over there and a scarcely illuminated level of darkness reigned. In a blur those windows flashed by the field of vision of old two-eyes, the line of sight was elevated above and beyond them into the somewhat farther distance, where, with a rosy gleam, with that quiet, mysterious pronouncement that is characteristic of any solitary light that appears in space, the constellation Forest Nymph had risen.

In the middle of the star, the troglodyte (he lives in dark caves, doesn't he?) saw the goddess, while his eyeballs, taking it all in, gradually protruded more and more and eventually sat out there on swollen, vein-covered stalks. In the silence that reigned all around she hovered out there, in a completely different world. The latter point was already evident for Julius Zihal; and here the certainty with which such instincts can lead to a crucial decision, even at a distance of two hundred paces, is worth mentioning. The star which the Forest Nymph inhabited belonged to a planetary system completely different from his own. Zihal knew that; the little he could make out, relatively indistinct as it was, was enough to convince him. He sensed — taking it all in all — that the surroundings in which the goddess moved, her customary behavior of an evening, her raiments — in so far as there were any — were those that belonged to a race foreign to him and of a superior station. And, insofar as he still rested firmly on his own tax office foundations, the latter still sufficed — even though weakened a bit — to protect the bureaucrat from the utopian notion of a leap across outer space, right down to the furthest and most secret depths of his consciousness; he did not even feel the gentle caress of such an idea. And so he took a sort of knightly vow — regardless of how little his demeanor and that of the Sixty-Sixer may appear to be knightly — he took a vow to consider the boudoir of a lady as a truly hallowed place.

For friends of such subtleties (but all of those things are just trivialities anyway) we mustn't shirk our duty to mention that the feeling for social distinctions that doubtless dwelled within Zihal prevented him, in this instance, from straying internally from the path of life's duties — entirely the same feeling that had protected him a priori from being taken advantage of by that vendor when he bought the Sixty-Sixer at the flea market.

However, from beneath the hovering presence of the goddess over there a breath of another sort drifted into the dark cave of the troglodyte and forced back the constructive chaos that was doing its work thoroughly there, illuminating, as it were, a single spot with a fleeting shaft of light. Indeed something else touched the bureaucrat, touched him just very gently, the way the thready breezes of Indian summer caress one's face: it was a beautiful thing to stand there in the dark and look so deep within and so far out beyond, it was beautiful even without . . . objects.

As if by some magical power of that word, darkness fell upon the constellation of the goddess.

11

But he was unable to relent and the breath of a new and different sort of order was repressed by a chaos, which, however, shaken out of its "concept," was momentarily unable to reconstitute itself. Loyalty to the concept failed in its duty. The grocer's pages, the writing pad, pencils, and lamp — they were lying around somewhere, dropped by a hand trying hastily to turn the focusing screw. Because in the end he did refuse to surrender himself to the influence of the Forest Nymph; the troglodyte, fleeing back into his dark caverns, now became a creature of hunger and the hunt, of the hunt that hunted in vain, laden with curses and gnawing hunger. A host of objects gradually revealed themselves to the one so recently obsessed with the totality of objects, be they ones newly risen, or ones not noticed previously by him. A distant, clearly and sharply illuminated window, for instance, like an echo of the Forest Nymph, like the complementary response to another color on the inside of a closed eyelid: green. Green clothing perhaps; it moved in a bright frame out there, far away. It looked tiny to him, as if the glasses had been turned around the wrong way, but of course not as sharp. It sat there off in the distance like something complete, like a bright, polished stone, but no individual details were revealed — impossible to say what was going on there or whether the intermittent disappearance or concealment of the moving green figure was due to a curtain or the door of a closet being opened . . . suddenly it seemed to Zihal that the case was taking on an objective character or considerable impressiveness: the green began to shade into white . . . now it disappeared again. He hastily turned the screw, pulled things in as close and sharp as he could. There was the green garment again. Gone again. Then, at a single stroke, everything went dark; immediately to the side, however, a new, dim light through a lowered shade. "Take aim!" came from the Sixty-Sixer.

The parallel-chambered gaze felt its way out there into the sooty, dark masses that went rushing through the field of vision of the glasses — now and then allowing individual elements of buildings that received light from some source or other to jump into prominence: protruding corners and spaces that, without the glasses, would have looked flat — the parallel-chambered gaze was reaching, in other words, for a substitute. Because there was, once having left the path designated by the Nymph, just that one possibility, namely, the finding of a substitute or . . . being suddenly locked up in that dark and confining room, sitting, so to speak, under a ventilating duct in an empty space. The bureaucrat's relentless charges against the increasingly impervious wall of darkness were like those of some tireless insect with a head full of huge eyes that bumps against the window pane over and over again, and like a buzzing fly, he banged — from the outside of course — against the weakly lighted, partially or entirely curtained windows of total strangers who were perhaps playing cards behind them, shaving, or still busy, late in the evening, washing the dog, if not finishing up some work with a jigsaw. Almost drowning in the ocean of featureless darkness, the bureaucrat was soon satisfied by the most cursory, oblique glance into any distant — not to mention dimly lighted — room, as long it was possible to confirm any movement around which his powers of imagination could wrap themselves; that alone sufficed to make the continuation of his strange activity possible. In order to improve the viewing conditions, he even climbed on a chair for the first time, and then, climbing up and down multiple times and pushing it back and forth, the bureaucrat spent half an hour doing battle with a curtain he never succeeded in seeing around — and that without ever confirming that there was anything there that had the character-istics of an object or that could be considered impressive.

As a last resort, there was Window III, with its open line of sight to the left. He now fell back on this reserve and as he moved forward again, two lately risen, not very distant islands of light beckoned to him, like a rescuing lighthouse to a sailor in distress. The nucleus of the one light was formed by a broad, white surface, and since the distance was not great, the bureaucrat was able to orient himself within the space over there, determine the exact location of the double beds, and improve his viewpoint by means of what at first was a provisional evaluation, then — after a slight change in position — a definitive ascent of the chair. So there he was, then, with the gate of his soul standing open, ready and well equipped, to take in the deeply offensive sight that offered itself across the way: each with folded newspaper, each illuminated by a bedside lamp. Faced with that despicable sight (which he himself and his spouse had once offered night after night, year after year, though that fact was not present in his mind), faced with low-grade foolishness of that sort ruining all his arrangements, there was absolutely nothing left to the bureaucrat other than to be proud of his bachelorhood. And at that point something quite curious happened within him, proving that even a pensioned bureaucrat of advanced years can be open to new experiences, namely this and just this: he thought to himself that he was a bachelor, living alone and actually a completely (in the trivial sense, of course) free man — he thought that literally: "a free man."To a certain extent, that didn't happen within him, but beside him, separated from him, without his grasping the situation properly (we, however, know better: he bumped against the little, closed sack, whose wall became taut). Still inundated by such a sensation, as if obliquely, from the side, he saw — and how that blow must have struck him, delivered totally unexpectedly and with full force! — a beautiful woman standing there completely unclothed in the second, still lighted window, like a vision hovering in space; what struck him there was a most resounding blow, like a slap in the face so hard it leaves a white spot. In the next moment, the light was extinguished over there. In the dark, however, exhaustion came over Zihal like someone's hefty body pushing everything else aside, and he gave in to it, overwhelmed and willingly, trembling slightly as he pulled off his clothing and slipped into bed.

12

The troglodyte Julius — we can call him that with justification, because he was only just then setting out on the pathway toward actually becoming a human being and having a history from then on; but at that point he was still possessed of thoroughly troglodytic character traits, like all those individuals in the myths who are spoken to directly by gods and in whose lives nymphs and geniuses of the sort go about their work in visible form — anyway, our troglodytic Julius slept like a log and even awakened in that form, that is, like a piece of wood that someone suddenly throws into the water. The Zadichek woman was standing in his room. Since she hadn't heard anyone moving, she had come in to check on him. The bureaucrat hastened to get himself ready and out into the kitchen for breakfast.

But wood floats on top of the water, even if it bobs under for a few moments. That he'd strayed from the "concept" yesterday didn't change a thing about the necessity of having that branch of the service and all the precepts that were valid within it. It was senseless and undignified to go on fleeing from them. Bow your head and turn back — neither thing easy, but, still, quickly and decisively carried out by the bureaucrat, now revealing in Zihal the outlines of what used to be called "bearing." Whoever has "bearing," of course, also has a feeling for proper distance and respect. Indeed, one comes to know and love him, that bureaucrat, while writing his pre-history, and at the same time, people of the cut of

Dr. Döblinger are more and more clearly revealed to be nothing more than nasty, ape-like specimens.

It points to a fine sensitivity, to a certain deep, inward gaze, to a feeling for appropriateness of the situation in one's own mental attitude of the moment, to knowledge of the possibilities of the mind for self-healing and correction — it points to all that when we now observe that Zihal once again sought support that morning in the Handbook of Administrative Practices. And not actually moral support. But, rather, as he let the highly refined material stream into himself from the ether-blue heaven where concepts dwell, eventually the same language responded from within him and the material condensed to transparent crystal again. And around such a configuration, the rest of the bureaucrat's personality could, to a certain extent, rearrange itself anew. He read the guidelines pertaining to the carrying out of the regulations in the Handbook of Administrative Practices concerning rank (§ 37ff.)

To All Departments:

(1) According to §39 of the Law of 25 January 19.., Gov't.Bull. Nr. 15, concerning the relationship of the State Civil Service Officers and the State Employees (HAP), the authorities charged with the direction of the various personnel departments (State Finance Offices, Purchasing Office, Central Administration of the Tobacco Monopoly, Office of Property Taxes, the State Lotteries, Trustees of the National Debt, National Central Bank, Court and State Printing Office, Central Mint, Central Authority for Precious Metals, General Testing Office) are required yearly to draw up separate lists, according to service branch and rank classification, of all officers belonging to their respective personnel pools according to the then existing organization of the service, based on the status as of 31 December, beginning with 31 December, 19 . . Within each personnel pool, a separate list is to be appended for each rank classification. The heading for a rank list will accordingly be worded, for example, "List by Rank as of 31 December 19 . . of the VIIth Rank

> Classification within the Personnel Pool of the Officials
> of the Legal Department in the Service Category of the
> State Finance Administration in Vienna."
> (2) Since listing by rank is solely for the purpose of
> legally establishing the order of seniority, only first and
> last names need be mentioned, and no other data. For
> the same reason, in those cases in which a category of
> rank contains only a single officer, the guidelines set
> forth in §39 HAP are no longer applicable.
> (3) The listing of officers is to be carried out with due
> regard to the regulations set forth in § 37 HAP.

And by this point he was already responding: "In cases of simultaneous occurrence and similarity of qualifications as regards spatial location, that view which offers the more advantageous conditions for visualization is to be considered as absolutely preferable, regardless of any lesser degree of worthiness of the object itself. In doubtful cases, the procedure should be carried out so that, among other considerations, those objects receiving the higher (absolute) evaluation take precedence, even if individual details of the spatial-optical situation in the competing case may be clearly considered to be superior."

Well, then — had the little sack burst? No, we daren't make such a claim. But order reigned in the sack. With the re-establishment of basic attitude and overall concept — by means of the magical effects of the Administrative Practices language — every new case would now be just another opportunity to apply the reaffirmed approach, a case in point, even in the face of the greatest aggregation of temporal-spatial conflicts.

And there was certainly no lack of those in the bureaucrat's new area of jurisdiction, as is already known. In good humor, he presently went after individual details and picked up — only now, and to us that appears to speak strongly for the still intact basic mechanisms of the Zihalian mind — the data lists on the grocer's calendar sheets that had been tossed aside yesterday, then spread them out according to their order of preference and started to evaluate them.

Meeting up with two significant difficulties in the most basic sense of the word — because he was attempting, from the very outset, to attribute a higher ranking to certain viewing sites, but was hardly able to base that objectively in terms of the impressiveness of what was concretely visible — the bureaucrat soon saw the entire structure of his rank-ordering cut across by another measuring standard which thrust through it obliquely from the side, so to speak, and divided it like a taut membrane, stretched as it were between the extreme opposites of the objectively rather low degree of impressiveness of the very first visualized image of the blond woman, Window I, opposite, (where it all started) which could maintain its position only by means difficult to grasp — across to that splendid example of womanhood suspended in empty, dark space, framed by the window (with which everything had ended yesterday). That horizon line, however, was occupied or illuminated by two stars, a rosy—pink one and a green one. Actually, the bureaucrat sank into his own inner visions for several moments, into a system of spatial coordinates that had its zero-point somewhere in the vicinity of his own navel, but whose so varied and yet confining dimensions astonished him with their varied categories of rank. We have no intention at all of denying the fact (even if the subject under consideration was Zihal's navel) that he was meditating. "At the very best he was brooding, that troglodyte!" some will object. However, it can even be claimed that the bureaucrat had very likely reached the point where real thinking begins and with that, even science.

Be that as it may, delicate intuitions slip away quickly, become blurred, and only their objects, preserving their hollowed-out external aspects, remain dependably beside our paths thereafter like hard milestones . On the following evenings, Zihal gave in to them totally and with that, even the security of the scale of their relative rank restored itself once more and the degree of impressiveness became subject to the various measurable indices of distance, illumination, and viewing conditions. And thus even the cases that conflicted timewise were gradually brought to resolution. Only from one side was there still some disturbance in the orderly evaluation of the material, one pole where things seemed to be pulled crooked or gathered up on the bias, as if one had grabbed a curtain with the fingers and squeezed: it was the already described vision at the termination of that first Sixty-Sixer evening — in other words just before Zihal collapsed in exhaustion — whose primal image he sought so obstinately without the least success. In fact, at one point he even put everything aside, even the "most impressive" and lurked in the left hand corner of Window III for over two hours, with its field of view into the black, fragmented depths off to the left. The good children down below there had gone to bed a long time before and were now lying in darkness after they had given the solitary man at the window cause to rejoice for a while. That revolting young married couple had long since found their way into their bedroom and immediately started paging through their newspapers in the light provided by their small, bedside lamps; and now even those had been put aside an hour ago and the lights turned off. And still the chains of Zihal's waiting had not been loosened. Every now and then, in order to bear them more easily, he'd send a glance over to the Forest Nymph who sent her solitary, rosy-pink gleam through space, loved and honored by the bureaucrat even if more precise observation had, in time, brought about a decrease in her value as an object of study. Because what the intoxicated eye at first took to be the surface of the goddess herself, bathed in rosy light, turned out to be her night clothes — a so-called pajama. We hardly need to tell the informed reader standing outside — outside of the little sack, that is — what happened with that splendid figure of a woman that the poor troglodyte was still looking for, right up to the end. That she could never be found again is probably quite obvious by now.

13

And so, with all that was going on, the bureaucrat's mood was divided and to a certain extent ambiguous as he went off to the Stammtisch the following Thursday, this time, curiously enough, resolved to go along to the café after eating. This time, he was immediately asked if he were going to do that — namely by Fräulein Rosl Oplatek, the Postmistress, whom he caught sight of immediately after he'd entered the small adjoining room where the Stammtisch circle met. In fact, he looked at her for a long moment as if she were sitting there alone and not surrounded by more than a dozen people. That Doctor Döblinger was missing was something that actually pleased the bureaucrat this time, considering his prevailing personal circumstances, but he was even more pleased when a place was made for him beside the Postmistress by pushing chairs together and he could accept her joking invitation that just for once, she'd like to sit beside a "real Councillor."

As his eyes sought some spot on the table cloth to hold on to — a starting place, so to speak, or a crystal around which the rest of his entire person could then arrange itself with decorum — the inner eye of our Julius (in the course of the narration, one just gradually comes to be on intimate terms with such a thing and calls it by its first name — every profession has its intrinsic risks, even the writer's!) — anyhow, the inner eye of our Julius was completely filled, indeed stuffed, overfilled, or, let's say clouded (the way a glass gets) by one last, remaining, echoing, yet in no way diminishing sensory impression; that emanated from the clothing of Fräulein Oplatek. This evening the Postmistress wasn't clad in green, but was wearing a brown skirt — the upper part of her outfit, her jacket, which was of the same color, Julius could see hanging on the wall — paired with a close-fitting, knitted sweater of sky blue color, which liberated a rather large piece of her broad, white neck and contained under tension the upper story of her person that began just below. While Zihal, with considerable — to a certain extent protective — circumspection, picked his supper from the menu, still using the action, so to speak, to collect his forces before marching out, rallying, falling into line, crystallizing, it so happened that she leaned over and pointed at his menu to recommend a dish to him; at that point, now, he believed himself to have been touched on the arm by half of her upper story. He felt that quite light touch — which was nothing more than being rolled into by a soft rubber ball — as something extraordinarily forceful, like a punch in the stomach, very nearly strong enough to demolish his uncompleted arrangements. Such unpreparedness, however, ran all through the bureaucrat on various levels, the crystal had shattered along several intersecting planes; there were indeed parts, but the whole, as such, was questionable. While eating he noticed that his hands were clumsy. A false impression might arise here — and we've deferred the matter in order to get this component into its proper place in the internal image of Zihal, because we can't do without it, it's part of the way he's constituted after all — however the false impression might arise that our Jules (good heavens, now we've ended up using a nickname — a worrisome sign!), that our Jules had become a young man again, in love, nothing more, his eyes simply full of throat, sweater, upper story. However, he was — and, what's more, feeling increasingly annoyed at the moment — actually preoccupied, turned inward, worming around in troglodytic caverns into which annoying, caressing breezes were constantly finding their way, drifting around like Indian summer, disturbing things. What mattered to him, however, was the path of duty in his life, making it secure. It wouldn't have taken much for his navel to spring into action again as the center for meditation and midpoint of a system of spatial coordinates.

On the way over to the café to which they later adjourned, the dark little troop of talking and laughing people down there at the bottom of the canyon-like streets was accompanied by the small and cold crescent moon in the waxing phase, which became intermittently visible high above the rooftops, lightly and transiently covered by a few wisps of heavenly cotton — thin strands, torn loose. Zihal, who was marching along beside his lady table-partner with decorum — quickly supplemented from his emergency supplies in the meantime — noticed that her gait, which the street lights accentuated and underscored at recurring intervals, seemed less resolute than her general appearance while dining, which had suggested strong foundations and an upright, rigid structure built from self-confidence, happiness, and the rest of the substantial blocks of her person — the almost certainly hand-knit sweater, her clean blond hair. Now, however, she seemed to be somewhat bent beneath the sky, yet simultaneously, in the movements of her ample hips, as if she were walking on clouds — indeterminate images, for Zihal at least, who considered it proper to leave all that to be noticed just out of the corner of his eyes.

In the café where they sat together in a smaller, more intimate group and where the first glasses of schnapps were soon being passed around, Zihal's mood was indeed improved — and that improvement had taken place in just a few moments. One can say that he regained his footing and was now pushing off from there once more. The bold warmth that was filling him came from a broad area of contact beneath the table which resulted from an entirely accidental movement on the part of his neighbor — and we mean it precisely: absolutely accidental, hand on the heart, no sneaky authorial thoughts, we're not trying to save something for later! — a bold warmth within Julius caused him not to perceive that contact as an extremely forceful, dangerous punch in the stomach, but as a benevolent force and an event that could be responded to. While they were drinking "white tie and tails" — as those little, open schnapps bottles used to be called in Viennese cafés — their conversation soon came around to grapes, and to Sievering, Grinzing, and the other villages around the city where they're grown. The billowing visions of the unknown latitudes there in the middle floors adjacent to him were strangely cut off within Julius by a sort of sharp wedge, which went through his own innards golden yellow, like wine, but whose point, however, was directed toward Fräulein Oplatek and the unknown. It was unavoidable that someone around the table would eventually suggest that there were warmer days ahead and they should make plans for a "Heuriger party," as the Viennese call their modest little excursions to those wine-growing areas on the edge of town, and the following Thursday was promptly decided upon. A decision in which the bureaucrat approved, especially since Fräulein Oplatek looked at him and laughed.

14

He stayed absolutely as long as possible. For that evening he had granted himself a leave from duty and went immediately to bed.

The following time was full of unrest. It came from various quarters, each inimical to the other, and managed to go running all over the bureaucrat's plans in the course of hostilities.

At one point everything was laid out in a temporal orientation, for the following Thursday; as a result, everything up to that date just didn't seem to be very enjoyable, never really turned out according to plan, even though things had seemed absolutely assured from the start.

In a second instance — coming from the opposite pole so to speak — the end result was the same: that demoness, whom the troglodyte had seen in all her splendor only for a few moments, prolonged her absence, but certainly did not let Zihal out of her claws, which reached out for him even if he just took a brief glance out of Window III into the featureless darkness in which the only thing which mockingly revealed itself was a bright rectangle with the two young people unrelenting engaged in reading their newspapers. That married couple was salt in the bureaucrat's wounds every time. And it was only with melancholy that he could watch the two young girls (Window III, view downward and to the right) when he considered that perhaps even for them, the future — as opposed to their girlish dreams — might not hold anything other than . . . reading newspapers.

The third unpleasantness, however, did not extend merely temporally beyond the following Thursday evening — which had doubtless been inserted as a welcoming island, but an island on which, nevertheless, even this time Zihal was not going to be able to set foot confidently and in full command of himself, but once again only with strangely fragmented impressions, isolated and ambiguously uncertain, a foreigner, so to speak, a foreigner in a confining sack — the third unpleasantness did not extend merely temporally beyond that Thursday (indeed, it actually increased, in the most concrete meaning of the word), but it had its source outside of and beyond the existence of our Julius, or, indeed of any earthly existence at all. But how greatly the life of that mythical creature, the Troglodyte, is determined by such forces, for instance, by a heavenly body! Because it was the moon, the moonbeams, the milky, silent light of the moon that turned into a strange sort of catastrophe for our Julius.

From day to day that heavenly body took on silent strength, and it was not merely in the gardens that everything bloomed, stretching up toward it; even dead matter — apparently or outwardly dead — the roofs with their tiles and metal or slate shingles rose up from their previous nocturnal, black flatness with more definite contours and more clearly defined gables. Here and there a tower protruded thin and needle-like, drawn out to a point that had been thrust even further beyond the common mass that was striving upward. This constantly recurring, changeable background of our existence, alternately rising and falling in bluish light and dark shadows, from which modern man lacks the power to take support and sustenance as he goes whirling along in the foreground of gaping space with his hasty, paltry, shadow dance — this background turned our troglodyte into a jagged, agitated silhouette, all the more agitated the more the moon goddess split open the cave where he'd been watching from side to side, like a spider in its net with its take-in-whatever-you-can eyes. Indeed, it seemed as if Artemis were actually hunting for him in particular with her arrows of light. Because the beams, like a glacier suspended in the air, slid into Window II and out Window III and laid a dripping cataract of ice exactly on that floor that looked suspicious to the bureaucrat, directly above the children with their touching, evening foot baths.

Yes, he was forced to bow down, deeply, then even more deeply, to the floor, until he was creeping around on all fours as befits the image of a troglodyte; indeed, he had to do his moving around almost on his belly, like a worm. Because in switching from Window II to III, walking upright was rendered impossible by the goddess who forced him down with incessant shafts of light that whirred down around him, making his figure stand out distinctly to anyone who might look over — indeed practically outlined it. The detour along the walls of his room, which really put his patience to the test several times — because in the midst of that careful creeping around, the totality of the objects to be looked at out there grew more and more gigantic and oppressive — that detour was made, in part, impossible by his own furniture, in part by the circumstance that on one side, he'd get into a broad moonbeam again, but in part it was also prevented by his own excitement, because of which he eventually knocked over, with a loud bang, a little table holding all his smoking accoutrements, which then compounded the deviltry by rolling around the floor, clattering and clinking. To his torment, he could feel the noise forcing its way through his open windows and spreading out into the stillness that reigned.

So — for the first time, he was finally forced to his knees groaning, our cave dweller, by the might of the goddess, then down on his face; and then he'd been broken, as the divine one willed, chased back from all his audacity into his true place as a troglodyte. He crept, obediently. He shot back and forth in his rooms like a rat, hounded by his objects, of which he had — something we consider quite noteworthy! — had enough, seemingly by chance, from the last moment he'd had to duck down like a hunter now chased by rabbits. It was a wild carrying-on. He could only climb over his chairs by slithering up from behind the bedposts, each time changing from a rabbit into a snake, as it were. And so, chased into the depths, actually through various animal forms, he became the prey one would expect to find on his sort of hunting preserve.

And, as we've already said, in great sufficiency. Right down to that young married couple who went on reading their papers unperturbed, everyone was bathed in patronizing brightness, visible in a totally voluntary way as they went about their evening's — or even nightly — activities. And, in truth, where they were previously lacking, Zihal could have stamped objects out of the ground, or, better said, conjured them out of his own eye, as he'd once done with that beautiful demoness. He no longer persisted in searching her out, but, rather — active everywhere — he'd actually succeeded that night in discovering three new subjects of the highest degree of impressiveness, whom he proceeded to enter into his catalog of stars in the adjoining room with the help of his pocket flashlight.

Did it not seem as if the treasure of still undiscovered object-totality were glowing mysteriously within the mountain, as if within those buildings, now bathed in a grayish blue cast, a greater fire were blazing up, already breaking out, here and there, through the increasingly numerous portals that began to light up? Were not the stars now beginning to rise? Was not the abundance of possibilities just now shimmering in its perfect completeness?

And, since the goddess had struck him with her arrows, thrown him to the ground, something else began to rise up within him: the whole fury of the chthonic underworld which now finally wants to be complete in its groveling, in its deep pain. Again it proves the presence of an organ within Zihal for what used to be called "bearing" when he now favored the rosy-pink star of the Nymph with just a single glance, in which there may well have been more defiance than reverent shyness. And — purely objectively and dispassionately — having convinced himself that his eyes were simply too weakly equipped to appreciate the individual details of the distant, green star, he even rejected that one in short order and removed it from further consideration.

As he crept around, his face with its little moustache broke through the dense moonlight as if through underbrush and not merely once, but several times, he thought he could feel the masses of light brushing against his cheeks and temples like cobwebs, like the caressing breezes of Indian summer. Isolation and loneliness grew above his shoulders like a dark, prismatic tower.

For Window III, the risk of counter-observation had always appeared so great that the bureaucrat — by day, Zihal was promoted to that status over and over again, so to speak — had relegated all candidates for observation from that spot to the very bottom of the list until further notice. However, certain new discoveries in the field of vision off to the left did not permit any procrastination; since the incomprehensible disappearance of the demoness, Julius had become suspicious and worried in regard to that part of his field of observation, as if anything else that might pop up there would not be able to be verified a second time. So here it was a matter of intervening quickly and decisively, of always making the most precise spatial and temporal determinations simultaneously; this was "to be considered urgent" (that's what he thought, literally). Finding sufficient cover at that post for Zihal to carry out the orders that he'd given himself was now only possible by squatting down so that his chin was about at the level of the windowsill, then propping his hands with the Sixty-Sixer on it. In certain cases, however, an upright posture, bending slightly forward, could not be avoided; here the size of the silhouette that one presented would have to be kept as small as possible by pressing very hard against the right side of the window frame.

Julius no doubt knew that it would be better to suspend all operations at Window III for the moment. But even though he knew that, he found himself getting involved there again and again, while his reasonableness and caution were propped against the wall like an umbrella that had been put aside. To Zihal's biographer, this point seems very important, indeed, absolutely critical within the life history of the bureaucrat, because there is no doubt whatever that Julius Zihal revealed the duality in human nature which occasionally asserts itself (and, as is known, is capable of becoming exaggerated to the point of illness in some instances). In other words, there is no doubt that Zihal himself was experiencing that duality in such an elemental fashion for the first time.

There he was, now, standing at Window III again, in a soft and — purely external — cloak-like feeling of himself, but simultaneously standing outside of himself with his common sense in some sort of unfruitful way, like a bare, scrawny bone that no longer belonged to his body. Those two, so very different and yet at the same time directly related, conditions within the same little sack were perceived by Zihal in a curious way — namely, a smile formed beneath his moustache. One might say, sourly in all likelihood. But the fact that he was smiling at all, sourly or not —

and not stupidly or vacantly — that in itself seems to us to prove that Zihal had another capacity, which he was perhaps revealing for the first time to that degree, that is to say, in such an archetypical internal state. One can make the most astonishing discoveries about a pensioned bureaucrat: this one for instance possessed the capacity for irony!

Its appearance indicates that the possibility still exists for restoration of equilibrium; however, should this last thread of humanity tear as a result of an extremely forceful punch in the stomach, then reversion to an animal state can occur — for instance in the interstellar space of fright.

It was precisely into the latter that Zihal was suddenly displaced. Too late for reason — now there was nothing at all left of that bone; things had . . . finally caught up with him. He felt that there was a certain validity about the event, yet at the same time wondered how it could be so, since it had really been anticipated and hence, in a manner of speaking he'd cast a counter-spell to ward it off...that interstellar space of fright was, strangely enough, not dark, but quite light, filled for the moment by the bright moonlight that passed right through the totally empty person of our Julius.

Directly opposite, where the flat, rigid, icy cataract of reflected moonlight flowed down the window panes, in the one casement window that now, with absolute certainty, appeared to be standing open, there was a definite movement — an eery one, to be sure, because something seemed to be creeping along the window sill, which by its very appearance totally excluded the calming, reassuring thought that it could be a cat. Even more — now it revealed itself to be a cylindrical or worm-like structure extending a little beyond the window sill, like the kind of feeler snails extend, but a lot bigger. And as a result, because its movements were slow, scarcely perceptible, and gradually reaching out toward Julius, the extent of its length was probably not obvious to his gaze because it was foreshortened when seen directly on; suddenly it gleamed in the moonlight, deeply and sharply. That flash from a polished, glass lens lighted the fuse of understanding of what was going on and its full implication for Zihal: a barrel was pointed at him. His barrels were pointed at that barrel. Nothing stirred; it was as still as death, as bright as ice. Unceasingly and soundlessly the two cannons fired away. But Zihal's flagship of total order took a direct hit first and went down.

Because, that he would ever go beyond that boundary — or even brush up against it slightly — which, like an invisible wall, separated and protected him from the simply unthinkable — indeed, unbearable, even just in his imagination — realm of ridicule, of scandal, of gossip in the building, not to mention a complaint or even formal charges . . . that he could ever even stumble across that boundary was, for Zihal, something out of the question, beyond possibility, beyond anything that was relevant to his life or could even be part of it, beyond anything that could even be contemplated. Even in that situation, of a purely external, cloak-like feeling of himself, bathed in it — bathed painfully, first with cold, then with strangely hot skin — he'd ended up there at that window over and over again, and even in that circumstance he was never assailed by doubts about the solidity of that dividing line — mask and wall. Now, however, this strange, solitary activity of his, carried on in deep caverns hidden from the outer world, had come into contact and conflict with the latter, and at the touch of a magic wand, there in front of him, like a new, oblique dimension, was a bridge between the inner and the outer worlds, in other words, what's called reality — as rigid as steel, no longer to be denied, even if still trembling from the force of the touch that had created it.

And so, under the cold and soundless fire of the enemy, the admiral's flagship went down.

It sank, centimeter by centimeter of course, still eye to eye, muzzle to muzzle with the enemy, until it was below the optical water line of the window sill, down to its knees, till under cover. From there, Zihal crept — in fact, with the movements of someone severely wounded — toward the middle of the room. The broad column of moonlight swam over to him, splitting around him to the right and left like rapids in a stream around the rocks, coiling around his cheeks and temples like the caressing breezes of Indian summer. Julius had lifted his head and turned his face toward the moon, at which he gaped with an expression of troglodytic idiocy and bright, flat, sliver-eyes, gaped questioningly, as if some regulation were about to be handed down from up there that would bring sense and order into his incomprehensible situation. But the goddess remained silent. And everything around him remained silent. Zihal stretched out on the floor, face down, no longer supporting himself with his arms, which lay along his side, slack as sausages. Past the low point that had been reached raced a torrent of imagination that demolished everything around it, leaving the wreckage to dance on his gloomy, angry back — the wreckage of the Tax Office, the wreckage of the vineyards out there with the hills dripping golden yellow, the wreckage of a green Postmistress, and a yellow shoe polish can.

A shrill, continuous signal sounded in the midst of the rising floodwaters, a ringing that seemed not to want to end. Outside, in front of his door, someone must have put his thumb on the button.

15

For the third time the bureaucrat showed his impressive side, indeed, his greatness. Every low point lends a certain momentary greatness by means of an offer of freedom standing right next to us, an empty saddle into which we can leap in order to gallop away from all of our fears and all of our troubles with the powerful gait of life itself.

Julius arose slowly and calmly. In the process, he majestically left the mad beating of his own heart lying on the floor beneath him. Standing in the dark, he straightened up his clothing, then walked slowly out in the dark, turned on the lights in the kitchen, went to the door and opened it — not just a crack, but wide open.

He found himself standing in front of a willowy, young, well dressed — elegant, actually — young man, who smiled, bowed twice in rapid succession, and gave his name: "Wänzrich, Wänzrich." He seemed to want to do everything twice, the first time for the sake of form, so to speak, the second time as if to apologize for pressing the matter, bringing it closer — his own person, for example. Zihal remained silent.

"I most humbly beg the Herr Councillor's pardon, pardon," said Herr Wänzrich quickly, "for this disturbance at such an unusual time of the day . . . nighttime, actually, nighttime. I will take the liberty of explaining . . . explaining everything to the Herr Councillor, if the Herr Councillor would be so kind as to just allow, just grant me five minutes' . . . five minutes' conversation." Julius, of course, felt that his own situation appeared to be somewhat less delicate and dangerous at that moment than he'd been all too ready to assume as he was getting up from the floor. Much more: the submissive tone of the stranger provided the bureaucrat with a redoubt behind which it was possible to withdraw for the present. But Zihal's pain was not lessened thereby, nor at the same time was his greatness, nor, as we have yet to see, his kindliness.

Zihal invited the stranger in. It turned out that he was wearing neither coat nor hat, in other words, appeared not to have come in from the street, but from the same building, and, of course, the bureaucrat hadn't really expected it to be otherwise. He motioned to one of the kitchen chairs, took one himself, and said, as a brief invitation to the other to speak, "Please." It was the first word he'd spoken.

Herr Wänzrich presented further details about himself by bowing slightly as he was sitting down and saying, "Wänzrich, Student at the Export Academy, world trade in other words. Wänzrich. I would like to take the liberty of approaching, acquainting the Herr Councillor . . . yes, the Herr Councillor, with a pressing but very modest request, not entirely without hope, without prospects of encountering sympathy, kind sympathy, understanding for my situation, that is to say, particularly from Herr Councillor. I have, you see, fallen extraordinarily — indeed, one could say, to a highly unusual degree — in love, I love someone, am in love. But there is suffering connected with it, great suffering, pains of longing, of yearning . . . of desire, yes. As an experienced man, an experienced man who knows life, yes, really knows it, has seen it from a position of responsibility, Herr Councillor will surely not be lacking sympathy for an immature and inexperienced person who finds himself in a situation of the sort."

Zihal was sitting leaned back somewhat during the hearing he'd granted to this supplicant during such odd, nocturnal office hours (at nighttime, at nighttime); Zihal was motionless, as if made of cast iron.

"Please continue," he said.

"Love engenders the great desire, the eternal wish — as people used to say in the elevated sense — if not for the impossible and currently unobtainable possession of the object of one's love (at this point the bureaucrat opened his eyes even wider and leaned back even farther), the object of one's affections, inclinations, of course . . . then at least for the sight of the object, that is to say, the person with whom one is in love, loves, cherishes, what I mean to say . . . if it were somehow possible, naturally, if the degree of clothing were such as to correspond to love's desire and as a result provide it with nourishment in a suitable way, nourish it I mean."

During all of this Herr Wänzrich smiled in the most ingratiating way, pushed each word confidingly across the table, as if he wanted to strongly urge someone to look upon it favorably, with favor, to really consider it understandingly, with understanding, to consider it favorably, just to be so kindhearted as to not reject it without looking at it.

"Well, then, it is the felicitous arrangement of the honored Herr Councillor's apartment in that regard, particularly the one, esteemed window of the Herr Councillor that faces to the rear, which brings me to my humble as well as pressing request, to request in other words, and in this I am emboldened by the surely not entirely erroneous assumption that the Herr Councillor, as I may be permitted to remark with all modesty and reserve, because I had opportunity, since the opportunity presented itself, that is, that the Herr Councillor, that is to say, as I may well assume, that the Herr Councillor would lend a kindly ear, would incline his ear, with understanding, understandingly, to such a wish on the part of a still thoroughly pure, still unrequited, young man still in the early stages of love for the maiden Margit, likewise pure. Considering that the object to which my love and affection are attached lives directly beneath me, since it's at the top of stairway number three, on the same floor as the Herr Councillor, that I live, have my domicile, my room and considering where Margit lives, totally in the same degree of purity as I, one can understand the impossibility of seeing the object of my affections from my window at the suitable time of day, actually nighttime, time of night, or actually of the evening, during the evening . . . in a state of dress consistent with love's desire, favorable to the development of affection, as long as the existing purity does not permit one to go any further; all the less so since a personal acquaintance has not yet been kindled, but perhaps still may be kindled. I moved into the room here just a few weeks ago, moved here, and right on the very first day, in the stairway, saw the sight that sent my heart and my higher impulses into turmoil, was permitted to look upon Margit, have looked upon her often since then, and not without hope on my part. First of all, however, the path to friendship has to be found, then followed in the proper and customary way, as is the case in any and all such honorable undertakings. For the impulses of love, however, to which I am constantly just about to — completely prepared to — surrender, a carefully arranged view one evening, in a state of dress doubtlessly suitable for strengthening the inclinations of the heart, would provide sustenance, would be sustaining in a salutary way, all of which would be possible from the esteemed rear window of the Herr Councillor. Margit lives with her younger sister, likewise pure, I know, and looking up from the street I have noticed that the blinds are not lowered in the evening, that the curtains are not pulled in the evening, not even when one presumes the state of dress conducive to sustenance, considering the time of day that is, actually of the evening . . . the evening. My request directed to the Herr Councillor is, accordingly, to permit me to look from the esteemed rear window of the Herr Councillor, a request all the more pressing considering the distress of a young heart in love, in the greatest affection, which does not have the unrealistic hope of anticipating understanding from the Herr Councillor . . . great and kindly understanding, from one with such knowledge of life and knowledge of such life and even such activities in general."

At those last few words Herr Wänzrich again smiled quite sweetly and, as it suddenly seemed to Zihal for just the fragment of a second, with a sort of glaring, naked impudence. His very large eyes, long and drawn-out in a somehow impudent, even obscene way, allowed the moist, gray-white of the sclera to show conspicuously and they were constantly in concert with hands which incessantly seemed to be submissively or humbly approaching something or other; and on the whole, for all of his overdone modesty, something seemed to be emanating from this person, something absolutely incessantly and continually probing, a feeling and grasping here and there by hundreds of tentacles — and it was impossible to fend them all off at the same time — which would eventually wear the other person down; something was always slipping through, unexpectedly creeping onto some spot or other of your skin, and even into your sleeves and while you were still trying to push it away, resolved once and for all to really grab and squash this audacity that was slithering around everywhere under other names and pretenses, it had, in the meantime, turned into a fat spider that was running across your nose and once again you'd realized it too late.

But within our Julius there dwelled nevertheless an old, very probably inherited, facility for rejecting this Wänzrich, for preventing any deeper sympathy for him from developing, superficially fascinated as he still might be by the suave and slender movements of the extraordinarily well cared-for hands, whose fragile wrists shot out of the cuffs of an elegant, soft, violet shirt with a curvaceous arabesque like the necks of snakes and then withdrew again — for such seductive feasts for the eyes coming from people who are incapable of developing a form of their own or (let's just simply say) their own life style and are hence always looking around for support in someone else's style — to such seductions that always emanate from people like that who seem to feel so completely well in their own skin, the bureaucrat was inaccessible. Because he himself possessed form and no one who knows him can argue the fact from this point on. That quite definite form had developed itself living on completely different ground, which could not be shaken even by Wänzrich's totally infamous bombardment of his nerves, despite Zihal's momentary — as already portrayed — extremely diminished condition. Behind this, of course, stood the deep violet wall of sonorous pain and with it, once again, a background and support for our sufferer, which was ultraviolet for a Wänzrich, that is, invisible, and would thus remain unassailable. Reduced to the simplest formulation, it could be said that Wänzrich gradually lost his composure because the answer to the question which he put to himself over and over while speaking so facilely — namely, where did the other person find such self-assurance under pressure that almost amounted to blackmail — because that answer eluded him more and more.

With Zihal there was actually something else, aside from basic structure, something empirical added from the external aspect of his life history: he had, certainly as a younger civil servant, and even as an older one, had to be available in his office for inquiries, complaints, and so on — please don't fall into the trap of saying something like "knowledge of human nature," because knowing or having learned something about that means one has had to look at it closely, or at least in passing. But what's involved here, in fact to a very high degree, is the extreme opposite of that, namely, the not-seeing of a person, the ability to see beyond a person. Any civil servant who tries to cope with large numbers of people during office hours with any other attitude than the one mentioned — a praiseworthy undertaking in and of itself — any civil servant, doesn't matter what sort, would be carried off to the insane asylum within six to eight weeks. To us, for example, all Chinese look the same at first (and all Europeans for the Chinese) and so do all members of the public to civil servants. So, instead of saying "knowledge of human nature" as you were about to earlier, just say something like "dehumanization." It's a protective maneuver of life, and also of the civil service. A type of callus formation, in my opinion. It provided a sort of secondary immunity to Wänzrich's neurotoxin; and so that foreground of callus still did its bit - along with something greater that served as a background: that incomparable fibrous rind around the soul left behind by any encounter with the public.

That array of silent powers had its effect and finally caused Wänzrich to fall completely silent. The agitated writhing of his countless tentacles gradually abated, the way they do with a dying jellyfish. He calcified, he underwent a change, he petrified. And, like the companions of Odysseus, whom the sorceress Circe once turned into swine on Aiaia, Wänzrich, too, was transformed, on this not any less mysterious terrain and by its unique powers. He became rigid; and finally there was really nothing left of him than a simple member of the public who's come in with a request or an inquiry, to whom one listens, whom one asks to wait for a moment, to whom one gives preliminary advice.

"Please wait here," said the bureaucrat curtly and went out. Actually in, that is, into his dark personal office, illuminated only by moonlight, shutting the door behind him.

He cleared his throat elaborately and with decorum; the party waiting outside could no doubt hear it. The consciousness of having won not only time to compose himself, but, already, the upper hand as well, confirmed his position before his primordial background and placed him once again under its standards, so that the darkness that had been forced back now surrounded the bureaucrat in a strong and sustaining hollow, the way a clamshell surrounds the creature within. There was no question of the Wänzrich affair remaining on the agenda for the future, let alone prolonging the bureaucrat's presence in his office now; no doubt quite seriously, but thoroughly composed in the attitude he'd assumed, he therefore — leaving Wänzrich in the waiting room (because otherwise the latter might have fastened on some other importunity, which could no longer be permitted!) — the bureaucrat therefore undertook something else, in the rear room, at II, without even so much as glancing at III.

In the distance twinkled the usually green or greenish star;

today, however, it was filled by a blue nucleus that moved suddenly — a nucleus or a soul in the sense of the innermost and central part of any item at all. The Sixty-Sixer's powers of attraction sharpened and refined everything to the limits of its ability, straining to overcome the distance, but then became overstrained, soon allowing things to become cloudy again. It was simply beyond its power. As if cast in glass, the tiny bit of illuminated space swam out there; now there was another bluish movement on the part of the tiny soul, but practically (as an object for viewing) it was as good as invisible, as good as not even present; yet at the same time one single bit of certain knowledge about the composition of the tiny heavenly body persisted — that its appearance was not being disturbed by a curtain or something of the sort.

Julius had to carry out his duty. The darkness, only partially penetrated by moonlight and the quiet all around him, the dignity within him, lying upon the darkness like a jewel upon black velvet, all of that made him inwardly more and more neat and well-combed, as if he'd bathed but not yet eaten, and had a cultishly empty stomach . . . he crossed his arms and remained standing in the milky stream of light, casually tossing aside earlier caution — it did not even enter his mind.

Only now did he proceed to evaluate the data which had led Herr Wänzrich to appear in the office. He walked into the adjoining room, examined the revised registry with the help of his flashlight, looked at his watch and shrugged his shoulders; only then, as a final check, did he take another look out of III, "view downward and to the right"— every window was, as expected, already dark by this time. He then made his way, the paper in hand, through both rooms and out into the kitchen.

Herr Wänzrich, who seemed to have spent the entire time sitting on the edge of his chair ready to leap to his feet, was visibly exhausted and put upon by being forced to sit quietly for a relatively long time; if he'd been able to move his ears the way rabbits do those spoons of theirs, he would have done so interminably in order to just have something, anything, moving — a tentacle, a feeler, or an organ of hearing. But, as it was, there was nothing left for him to do but use his knees for a piano keyboard, because to walk back and forth in the kitchen was inconsistent with his professional, one might almost say, good manners and re-strained bearing toward the bureaucrat. Well, at the latter's entrance, he spun around toward Zihal with his hands on his knees as elegantly, as oiled and easily as if he'd been stuck on a spindle, and, as a continuation of the same motion, rose to his feet and bowed, with a bow, by means of which he threw himself quietly and anew upon the good will of the master of the house.

The bureaucrat, holding the page in front of him with his right hand, took only a single step toward Herr Wänzrich, without bothering to return his bow. A quick look at the kitchen table allowed him to recognize with considerable interest the nature of the object that was lying there, but all he did was furrow his brow slightly; it was a short — perhaps only two hands long — black telescope, a sort of spotting scope, as they used to say. So it had already been brought along! The bureaucrat never finished think-ing out the sentence in which the little words "still and all!" occurred. Then he announced the following to Herr Wänzrich, repeatedly pulling out his pocket watch and glancing at the piece of paper: "The case you wish to investigate further is no longer available for examination today. Nevertheless, you have my per-mission. Should you wish to avail yourself thereof, you are to appear here promptly tomorrow evening a quarter of an hour before the time appointed for the case in question, which is ten o'clock, and announce yourself with two short rings of the bell. I thank you."

All tentacles fell into a violent, quivering movement, while Herr Wänzrich expressed his thanks equally rapidly amidst many bows. Zihal preserved stony calm and imperturbablilty. "No need to thank me — that's what I'm here for, " he said coolly. And with that customary, polite bit of officialese, which still and all might perhaps not make proper sense at that point, the bureaucrat closed the door behind Herr Wänzrich.

16

On the following morning — it was draped in a gray and driving rain — Zihal had only to cover a relatively short and easy road back to composure and bearing. The highly refined administrative practices material trickled down from the ether-blue heaven where concepts dwell and onto the ground without encountering any resistance, then rose again — thoroughly changed in outward aspect and content, of course, but in spirit and tone, however, the same — like fluid from a spring. Julius read:

> A Civil Servant, who, as a result of illness other than those designated in § 62 para. 1, has become totally disabled, through no fault of his own, prior to the completion of five years of service (Article 5 of the Pension Regulations of 14 May 1896, Gov't. Bull. Nr. 74, revised version) may claim pension benefits of unlimited duration in the amount of one fourth of the last recorded salary level, with a minimum amount of 800 Crowns, regardless of whether more favorable treatment would have resulted from the application of § 62 para. 4. If the Civil Servant has contracted the illness resulting in total disability while on active duty, additional benefits may be granted by his administrative superiors.

Such sad words, such a serious matter — it all fit with the day's mood; a talented person always knows where to position himself, where he'll be most productive at the present moment, find some sort of intellectual stimulation or be edified.

But beyond that, the case appearing for consideration today before his reestablished inner form was not an easy one, that is, the one concerning the scheduling and regulation of the Wänzrich affair. Zihal fell into a lengthy deliberation and only after he hit upon the following formulation for the purpose of modifying the entry on the revised registry under "Window III, view downward and to the right," 10:15: "filed under suspended activities category for the present, simultaneous with suspension of counter-observation."— only then did the affair seem to him to have been put in its proper place.

He felt the urge to go out, but strangely, as he arose from his desk, a certain stiffness and tiredness attacked him in the small of his back and he had the indistinct, overall feeling that his body was not in its usual working order. The latter stood there as a hindrance, as a dark ring around Zihal's revised intentions, which the previous evening had sharpened to a more definite point. But he finally took his hat and coat and a warmer scarf and left. In the stairwell it seemed to be rather cold. It was hardly a good day for going out. From the very beginning, it was like walking into a funnel, toward its constantly narrowing apex, from which Zihal consistently and increasingly shied away, as if from some rather gentle but persistent force which he couldn't make stand still or grasp, just as little as he could Herr Wänzrich's tentacles and as little as one can grab hold of the thready breezes of Indian summer, when they billow before the expansiveness of fall like a huge spider web that you run into with your face because you can't see it . . . He walked across the broad Ringstrasse near the Imperial Palace, into the inner city, past all those spacious parks and imposing buildings which always embodied for him an overall concept (Grand Dwellings or, actually, the Temple of the Double Eagle) beneath which his life had proceeded, wrapped in it like the earth in its firmament — though the bureaucrat was not endowed with any direct affinity toward those solemn examples of petrified architectural flatulence. They were necessary; that means, they were simply . . . the state itself, just that. He himself basically loved the water faucets of polished brass in the modest stairwell of his building much more; they were necessary, too, which means that they were simply . . . life, that was all. That was something that could only go on its way in the outlying neighborhoods. Here, on the other hand, absolutely everything belonged to the state, not just the Reichsrat, the Parliament, which stretched out on its side with its columns like fat arms that seemed to flutter past one's eye; not merely the Imperial Palace, which, with its green roofs, was set back from everything else by an immoderate distance according to the standards of city dwellers, leaving an inland sea of space rolling away in front of it — no, even the imposing private palaces, with their doormen and equipage in front, and even the well dressed people who were quite simply getting around on foot, and beyond that even the show windows of the sizable and more luxurious stores — all of that seemed to be constantly in costume and standing in front of the footlights, all staged and subsidized by the state; but in doing that, it departed from its ether-blue concept heaven in a dangerous way and, with its broad, swirling front of buildings, showplaces, and persons — private of course, but of a quite doubtlessly higher order — came flooding down upon the bureaucrat and upon his revised intentions. Those intentions soon led him, let's say, into the "Graben" with its beautiful Plague Column and into still other places, toward the fronts of sparkling, neat show windows of certain stores to which he'd never previously paid any attention; sparkling and neat to an especially high degree simply because everything that an optician spreads out before us — the eyeglasses, the lorgnettes, the loupes, the binoculars — even the curious "Trieder" model — and, finally, the telescopes with their extended tubes — emanates completely from the eye, that is, from the purely idealistic conception of the eye and what is associated with that is clean, crystal clear, mirrorlike, unbribable.

Those professionals whose job it is to build showcases have, of course, long since discovered what's crucial and hence the whole tone is one of extreme neatness and sleekness from the very start, and anyone looking in comprehends immediately that the instruments sitting there on transparent glass shelves or standing in front of a background with just the faintest tinge of blue or gray have something to do with one of the most enticing things in the whole world, namely, with light, which they take up with their crystal-clear, undeceivable eyes, collect it, lead it on, or refract it. To put it in general terms, it is the glassy physiognomy of abstraction that's looking at you there, a chamber of abstractions open on the street side, rather cold — not really cold psychologically or physiologically, but in the astronomical sense; with one of the larger tubes of that sort, you could even keep watch on the stars.

Yes, one can; and Zihal knew that, too. More than that . . . he knew that it was within his power to acquire such a telescope, in other words, that the stars were within his power, to a certain extent, within the grasp of his wishes, that some day, no . . . evening ˙. . . or actually, at night, at night, he could put an end to their haughty distance and their ambiguous, standoffish blinking, green and blue. He had the funds to buy such a scope, even one on a neat, polished tripod that could be swivelled in all directions. And with that, a sort of dictatorship, a total, uninhibited domination by those greedy, roving eyes over a broad area (indeed, it could be called an entire section of his district of the city!) would be established. Even the Forest Nymph would have to climb down out of the sky, pulled out of the mysterious depths of space, pulled nearer — and profaned! And profaned. Something like an attack against all fronts was taking place within Zihal. Was it also one against the path of duty in his life, in other words a revolutionary action, or was that path of duty only now going to be brought to its complete greatness and dignity by being carried out to its boldest extent?! We're going to see that both were true.

Zihal was cognizant of the significance of what he was about to set in motion — if not right at the moment, then sooner or later — by the purchase of such a telescope and, to be sure, not in a purely external, cloak-like way, but with the greatest intensity. That such a deed — weighty in itself and clearly underscored in its weightiness by the purchase price of several hundred crowns — that such a deed had to have consequences, had to lead to a point, perhaps even to breaking that point, but in any event, in a totally daring way right into the narrowest portion of the funnel's mouth — he felt all of that and yet, at the same time, it exercised a powerful attraction. With it he would be committing himself, with it he would be developing a more powerful organ of personal destiny than had been the case earlier with the Sixty-Sixer, the purchase of which, even back then, had been perceived by him as the beginning of a new segment of his life. A powerful organ, protruding gigantically from his person, from his life, one that couldn't be overlooked, defying nymphs and goddesses! A weapon which — if it came to that — could gain the upper hand with the warrior himself, eventually tearing everything into shreds.

Not a time to be miserly. All that remained was for him to bear, figuratively, the weight of the impending deed in order to bring it into the world; and so he alternated back and forth several times between the two or three largest optical shops of the inner city, spending long moments in front of their show windows, deep in study.

No faintheartedness, no beating around the bush now; it had finally come down to inquiring about the prices, which were not visible on the larger of the instruments on display in the show windows. This was the moment when the affair had to attain some sort of reality, at least in the form of more specific information: he would find out how much money had to be taken from his savings account. But nevertheless, even if Zihal already had the money with him, the situation had in no way ripened to the point of a purchase; the general attack required a certain latitude to develop and finally reach its proper cadence; only then would that point be reached. This was not simply a matter of hesitation. He possessed an inner sense of form, our bureaucrat, quite thoroughly. Something Herr Wänzrich found out yesterday.

The large glass door of the shop, as clean and absolutely transparent as if it were an enchanted, solidified piece of air, opened before Zihal into an atmosphere inhabited by the absolute and final sterility of things crystalline, of a world dissolved down to its very last fragment into diopters, angles of refraction, lenses and anastigmats. If the show window had already proclaimed that, even if only superficially and, so to speak, unidimensionally because of the dirty street on which it fronted — here the same form of existence extended out into spatial dimensions on all sides, a tidy but foreign race constructed of only two basic elements, in inexhaustible variations: the black of the tubes and the crystalline or watery, round gaze of the lenses.

In stores of the sort, the service is always especially polite, whether you're bringing in a prescription for eyeglasses or want to buy a pair of opera glasses. You're not dealing with the usual shopkeepers but with specialists, advisors who really know their way around in their workshops as well. Out of a shop on a side street, an optician — and there are, for example, some who carry the title of "University Optician" — can practically create an anteroom to the temple of science.

Zihal sensed all of that the moment he entered; and it was noteworthy that he responded to it by allowing his formal side to predominate immediately. He totally and completely ceased to be a private person, as it were, something which came out in the way he talked as, standing in front of the gleaming glass surface of the showcase, he now announced the following: that he was considering the purchase of one of the larger sized telescopes, but for today wished merely to be instructed briefly about their specifications and prices. And it had to be an instrument that could be used in the dark — adding that because it seemed important to him.

17

In the afternoon we find the bureaucrat once again in the inner city, feeling better after his postprandial nap. And, as a matter of fact, the weather had improved as well; it was still rather gloomy, but no longer wet and rainy. Zihal had paid a visit to a second, large optical shop, and there too, was standing in front of a spacious wall case whose sliding glass door had been opened, studying a row of tripod-mounted telescopes whose barrels were all pointed in the same direction, like a herd of geese whose heads have suddenly become immobile. The telescopes, arranged according to size, potentiated and exaggerated their individual natures in the eye of the beholder, which made a tempting impression on the bureaucrat. "Is the instrument to be used for terrestrial observation or in relation to the hobby of astronomy?" asked the friendly expert. But Zihal didn't quite know what to make of that question and you have to admit that its precise answer, seen from his perspective — from his world of concepts, so to speak — would have been difficult, because he would have had to use the paradoxical term "terrestrial astronomy." And so Julius said, "As far as

possible, the instrument should be adaptable to both purposes."
After the salesman had handed him yet another catalog and price
list, similar to the one he'd gotten that morning and was still
carrying with him, the bureaucrat walked out into the street again.

He may really have been feeling better since his afternoon nap;
the fragile feeling in his clearly no longer youthful bones and the
slight feverishness that he'd noticed as he got up from his desk
earlier had disappeared for the moment. So, no longer hindered by
the frailty of the body, his perception of the significance of his
position — not to mention the momentousness of the situation —
could spread out more easily within him, animating him, exciting
his cells, and swirling the freshness of the external world all
through the inner one. Now he clearly recalled his previous walk
past the red, crenellated fortress, when he'd bought the Sixty-
Sixer; between that point — with regard to time, not really very far
back — and today lay a whole tangle of events, the likes of which
had never occurred previously in the bureaucrat's life — a life
whose stations had already begun to resemble each other, just as all
railroad stations do. But here they no longer seemed to fit together
at all the way they usually do after you cover a short intervening
stretch of tracks — even quite apart from the increased size of the
optical instruments, which really only represented the most superficial difference.

And so he strolled through the city; even that was quite unusual.
He was carrying around a purpose that trilled and fluttered within
him, an affair (well, what're you supposed to call it anyway —
basically such things are just trivialities), a sensation, a heightened
awareness of life and, with that, a curiosity about it, and with that,
in turn, youth — indeed, nothing less than just that. He had, on the
whole, lived without sensations, had actually sat patiently and for
years in his own emptiness as if in a still puddle which reflects the
sky, without even realizing that it's the sky — and a few blades of
grass hanging over the water as well. He'd never realized that there
was a way out that led through sensations, into which one at first
stumbles by chance, but then looks for and finds, then eventually
incorporates it within himself and can no longer do without it. And

in this way and absolutely no other do things lead to the bulk of the so-called "experiences" of men and women today. No, the puddle was just accepted, it was legitimate; sitting in it, surrounded by water, one would never get to the point of thinking that the water was just standing there, that it should really be flowing. As long as people, in the beginning of this newest of all civilizations, were still inured and tolerant toward their own, already present emptiness, and endured it patiently like a roommate, considered it legitimate, just that long was it impossible to draw the basic, inherent consequences from that civilization, achieve its real power, and put the null point decisively behind.

But that not yet displaced null point (not displaced, as well, in the sense of there still being an open pathway) wandered there through the beautiful streets, which, of course, were well-known and familiar to him from his youth, but totally as the setting for another sort of life than the one which he was leading — one he didn't even wish to lead. His equilibrium was not disturbed by an unusually forceful cluster of external influences; nonetheless, he felt it necessary to bring to people's attention that, for instance, he'd been to Paris as a young man and, accordingly, felt justified in remarking, under certain circumstances, that his own native city had a certain inner kinship and deep-seated similarity with that western metropolis. Not everyone who was walking along there — even if more highly placed — could consider himself an eyewitness to such affairs. He was, the good Herr Councillor, objectively — that is, looked at from the outside — quite alone among the flashing lights that were beginning to cut into the evening and a certain — connected with big cities, it would seem — undue haste. Old boy, pensioner, bachelor, off on his adventures, and not even trivial ones at that. They were complicated enough; and he was making them even more complicated by pursuing them systematically.

Here, as he walked down a street that descended to the Danube Canal, swarming with people and vehicles and stretching off through rows of bright lights into the deepening, smoky evening, here, for the first time, he was struck quite unexpectedly by the counterthrust which responded to the general attack just getting underway, like a very sharp wedge, golden yellow, across the entire moving front. Zihal looked up in astonishment, as if this were coming from outside, catching sight of the sulphur-yellow portal of the evening closing between the clouds above an opening where a street intersected from the left. For the first time the already very much enlarged sack, in which Julius was still caught, was being worn out of doors; it had become comfortable, like a suit that you walk around in every day — pressed quite closely against you, so to say — and he felt the sides of it again, compelling him to stand or walk beside life, to think and make plans, but separated from life by a completely transparent, but unyielding, membrane. The fact that, if the weather were to improve in the next few days, he would be going on the trip to the vineyards that they'd all planned and to which he himself was looking forward — and yet, at the same time, inwardly he couldn't see himself doing it (literally, the bureaucrat thought, "Under such circumstances?") — anyway, that trip to the vineyards, here, now, put down right beside him, close to him, abruptly seemed like a monstrosity, indeed quite impossible. All of that, of course, just for the blink of an eye. He felt pain, but that remained with him somewhat longer, like a sound slowly dying away or a persisting, but diminishing, image in complementary colors behind the lid of a closed eye. Here, after the general attack that had transiently exhausted him, our bureaucrat took his very first look at his own entrapment and imprisonment and recognizing them as such, managed to pull off the trick — and this must have represented something totally new for him — of standing in the sack and simultaneously looking at it, and with that found himself at the beginning of the possibility for personal progress, personal fulfillment.

During his internal exertions — which simultaneously made him inhale the premonition of a previously unknown form of work — he'd barely managed to take several slow steps forward on the sidewalk, but hadn't been run into or bumped despite the crowds, as if some good fairy had erected a magic wall around him to protect him from any disturbance. Now, as his inner tension subsided, everything sank into the mousy gray of the deepening evening and the bureaucrat again ended up on the level from which he'd just ascended; there it was in front of him and, of course, occupied by the very things he'd imagined — for the moment by the herd of black, goose-like tubes with outstretched necks. Now he stepped out briskly, toward a large café that he'd seen there and had decided was appropriate to the unusual circumstances, ran into someone, excused himself, was then bumped into himself and, likewise, asked to excuse the offender.

And so Zihal landed in a large room with a lot of gold and mahogany on the walls and a very snooty and arrogant race of upholstered chairs and settees which had spread out in all directions — luxurious in and of themselves, but from the purely functional standpoint, dedicated merely to people's more or less attractive backsides. All of that made no impression on the bureau-crat, not even a "more highly placed" one, nor even one related to the "Double Eagle of Our Nation." A sure instinct within him refused to dignify all that ostentatiousness. He put the catalogues and price lists down next to his coffee cup and his cursory, com-parative study of the documents quickly revealed a high degree of similarity of both firms' offerings, the prices of which corres-ponded in every instance. But what really kept the bureaucrat from observing or critically registering the scene and everything that was going on there was not simply the subject with which he busied himself — even though an agreeable, nervous tension about the choice was beginning to develop from studying the precise descriptions, the illustrations and the price lists — but rather, despite all that, it was the continued echo, the afterglow of a sense of inner disturbance resulting from a perception of space that seemed to be centered out there above the opening of the side street where the long since extinguished, yellow gate of evening had been located, but then again, emanated from there, as it were, distracting the bureaucrat from his objective studies like a care-fully aimed beam of light. Beside that, everything within him and in front of him seemed muted and wrapped in mousy gray; for several moments the situation included the sort of comforting feeling that one has when one feels a little feverish and finally decides to go to bed, where the covers permit the somewhat fragile and shivering body to withdraw luxuriously into itself.

18

Herr Wänzrich arrived punctually. Zihal received him icily but with the greatest official correctness, showed him to his place, acquainted him with the elements of the most suitable position for viewing, and paid no further attention to him. The overcast sky hid the moon — now, of course, when there was no longer any danger of counter-observation. Zihal smiled bitterly in the dark. He had simply considered counter-observation as part of the price that he had to assume, integrating it to a certain extent with the rest. And suddenly, in that connection, by extension of that possibility, he now saw his room there full of people crowded around the windows, nonchalantly sticking out their long tubes in all directions; it was as if the room were filled by a gigantic, spectral hedgehog whose barbs protruded rigidly into the open — an optical underbrush, the integrated counter-observation that would relieve him of all his worries, but which would not even leave a space as big as a crack for him to make his own observations. At the same time it became to clear to the bureaucrat that he was beginning to think in a new and, for him, unheard-of way; furthermore, for a fraction of a second he seriously thought he could see a way to take care of the entire problem.

Herr Wänzrich was now getting ready to fire and was hastily turning the various screws on his hand-held cannon. In the dim light, one could almost see the countless tentacles of that repulsive creature waving every which way in excitement. Suddenly — obviously he seemed to be right on target — happy little squeaking sounds could be heard, like the whinnying of a tiny horse, and at the same time Herr Wänzrich took up a shaking or slightly hopping movement: he was doing a little tap dance of happiness with his feet.

Repelled, Zihal turned away from that person who, totally filled with his one and only preoccupation, was boiling over like milk on the stove. Basically he hadn't expected anything better from Wänzrich when the latter, the object of his observation having finally fallen into darkness after some considerable time (the dear children, as we already know, certainly didn't hurry getting ready for bed), immediately took his leave of the bureaucrat with numerous bows and expressions of gratitude, accompanied by violent tentacular movements. It clearly never entered the mind of that subaltern individual to broaden his horizons, for instance, by wandering through the other deeper and more extensive star-filled galaxies with the help of an expert. He just went running after his stupid infatuation. He was totally undignified. His permit should be revoked. Too bad he'd just made the brief comment, "You do have a permit, you know" when Wänzrich, still obsequiously taking his leave, asked ten times whether he might come again. But, of course, it could be withdrawn, anytime, in the same way it had been granted; to make it valid for a definite period of time was totally out of the question with Wänzrich. But the bureaucrat, benevolent person that he was, had gone a step farther on the occasion of Wänzrich's leave-taking, or, to be precise, a step too far: a small, slightly inviting movement of his hand in the direction of Window II and words to the effect of, "In addition, if you're interested . . . " And that was already enough for Herr Wänzrich to send a fat spider of impudence, an invisible and uncatchable one, across the bureaucrat's face. "Oh, I do indeed most humbly and obediently thank the Herr Councillor, am overwhelmed with gratitude to the Herr Councillor — however, all of that (he tentacled in a vague and yet belittling way toward Window II, as if he didn't mean just it, but a whole floor, a whole group, a whole category of experiences), all of that, such things, pleasurable things, pleasures, are entirely out of the question for me, such observations. But nonetheless a great deal of pleasure, I wish the Herr Councillor a great deal of pleasure." And with that, he was gone. And Zihal was left with a deep-seated, subtle, and gnawing rage, very similar to that which may be experienced by an artist who unintentionally gets involved with a dilettante and notices too late that the dividing line between the two classes — fine as a hair, deep-seated, and not outwardly identifiable — has already been completely crossed.

Zihal entered his observatory again. But that he would have a much freer hand there from now on — he just couldn't bring himself to thank Herr Wänzrich for that at the moment! — and turned his attentions toward the tiny,distant greenish-blue star, in so far as that was possible with his unsatisfactory instrument (wasn't the resentful soul of the Double Eagle in there dreaming, wasn't it secretly plotting revenge for its impending demotion?!). He took aim at the — with regard to position — somewhat more highly situated star, which, of course, wasn't saying much at such a great distance, since the individual details remained obscure in any case. However, when drawn closer by a telescope, that slight elevation of "Greenish-Blue" could lead to considerable difficulty in observation and thus it became advisable to gain a line of sight such that one was more or less on the same level with the window sill out there.

For that it would be sufficient, as Zihal had long since figured out, to climb onto a chair. However, aside from the fact that a modest elevation would only be of slight advantage — but a very basic one!— in the standing position, it would be impossible to use an adjustable telescope on a short tripod (the only kind that could be considered if one wanted to remain at proper height and on target during prolonged observation). Resting the scope on the window sill was out of the question because it was too narrow and wouldn't have satisfied the positional requirements in terms of elevation, quite aside from new danger of counter-observation because of the protruding tube, even if that didn't have to be looked upon as inevitable at Window II, but rather, at worst from further to the left; still it had to be taken into account.

Accordingly, what presented itself for consideration was the necessity of procuring a table that offered sufficient space for the observer's chair on its surface, as well as a small end-table that could be placed in front as support for the short tripod. In that regard the little smoking table could be considered suitable, even if there was a certain amount of distrust toward that piece of furniture because of the noise it caused a bit ago. The smoking accoutrements located on top would have to be removed and locked up ahead of time a) because of their complete superfluity, and b) because of the commotion caused previously, which, in the event of a repetition or relapse respectively, would be subject to prosecution. Perhaps that was the way to proceed, combined with the immediate withdrawal of Herr Wänzrich's permit, for which, in view of the new arrangements that had to be made, there appeared to be a clear indication.

But the final dispensation was based on the fact that no suitable table was available, aside from the big one in the kitchen, normally under Frau Zadichek's jurisdiction — which could lead to unpleasantries, quite aside from the problems of transportation and the offense which the bureaucrat might take at this unusual transfer (which he would only have been able to achieve with considerable difficulty, alone and in a darkened apartment). Accordingly, there was already justification for the purchase of a table and specifically, a table produced by a suitable craftsman in a way consistent with its intended use — simply, without a glossy finish or any of the usual decorations. The cost would be added to that of the telescope as an accessory and hence both would be covered as a single item.

19

The bureaucrat's increased authority now led him to carry out the tasks related to his new area of responsibility during some mornings; and the evenings went by quickly as well. In addition, Herr Wänzrich still remained in possession of his permit for the time being and night after night he carried on in front of the window in the same ridiculous way as he did the first time. All Zihal could do was to pity the man more and more: he was simply glued, in the most confining way, to one and the same object which long since, namely at the final revision of the registry according to rank carried out by Zihal, had been relegated to a much lower position than the one the bureaucrat, initially somewhat overwhelmed, had considered proper when he drew up his first inventory.

We've already mentioned the fact that the bureaucrat, in his very talented way, knew how to take on strength by imbibing the highly refined administrative practices material from the ether-blue sky where concepts dwell, always from the very concept-locales to which he felt an affinity at the moment, depending on his mood and circumstances; and that he found them, those proper spots in the ether-blue heaven, where they did not remain purely abstract and rigidly arched but could descend upon him in a looser (more human, one is almost tempted to say) fashion — that was Zihal's real talent. And it also reveals itself in the fact that he no longer understood that heaven in a subaltern-literal way (and less and less so in recent days), but increasingly independent of the specific point of reference or content of those celestial administrative procedures, and now in full possession of his newly won inner form, applied them to entirely different situations, freely chosen by him.

He read just that one book. We've learned earlier that he, as a serious person, rejected the reading of novels, for instance (and in that regard he mentioned another justification to Dr. Döblinger, which we'll hear about later). He read just that one book — but he knew how to use it; and that alone we consider decisive. For him that book was a useful tool and not some cultural plus to be added to others, a sorry and at the same time silly role that the best works of literature are often forced to play by their readers. Zihal, on the other hand, had the ability to dissolve those almost totally hardened concepts that were in the book, to make the buds from which they had once come swell and burst into flower a second time, to repeat their development to a certain extent, but with regard to a different subject matter. And in that way he developed form, arrived at an inner configuration. To put it differently, he was able not merely to assimilate the concepts that were offered into the physics of his cognitive function as unchallenged convictions but could also cause them to trickle down and have their effect on a lower level — that of the chemistry of his most personal life. He was able to turn a conviction into a personal quality, that is, not only to know something, but to dissolve that knowing in the warmth of his life to such a degree that it came loose from its subject and, thereby, as well, from any connection with cognitive function — now it just floated off freely to attach itself to a subject of its own choosing.

Without doubt, that alone is character development, and the bureaucrat was laying its foundation within himself in the best way possible. He really understood how to use *his* book; and that's already saying a good deal. Today, such an obvious fact is only in the possession of those few people who still know that the subject matter of one's reading material is completely irrelevant, because for the human spirit, a book is no more — and certainly no less!— than a runway is for an airplane. If, taxiing along the lines, it can take off from them, then eventually separate itself from the entire page and float freely, perhaps more freely and liberatedly than the author, then the latter has at last, and in the best way, received his final, most superficial and secondary reward — that of effectiveness. Because he's gotten someone to imitate him; indeed, perhaps he's even been surpassed, at least at that place in his book, on the page where the reader took off from the literary runway. Can a writer wish for anything more, with regard to effectiveness, than to bring about a change, a transformation through something he's conveyed carefully and restrainedly with his prose? And as an aside: only technicians and concierges want to pay attention to things all the time, constantly want to be sure about something or other.

The stature which the bureaucrat had gained thanks to his extended goals was reflected in his choice of excerpts from his book; and in retrospect, the inner city through which he'd so recently strolled, with those gigantic dwellings of the Double Eagle — not inhabited at that particular moment or, for that matter, at any given moment at all, like all the empty palaces of important personages who were spending their time in similar ones somewhere else, while their splendid, deserted rooms here dreamed on behind closed blinds — all of that, the buildings and the more highly placed personages, no longer seemed so unimportant, so foreign, so lacking in attractiveness. A capacity for greatness began to develop in Zihal and he was already capable of relating previously unrelated things to each other under a warm covering of sympathy. But secondly, what he took away from his book today (and almost without hunting for it — it opened to the proper page on its own!) was something that was more in line with a kind of resolute sternness, a — if one has to say it — punitive seriousness as well, like something borne by a distant, booming voice rolling out of the interior of a spacious edifice.

At first he read various passages concerning an area whose subject matter and content were certainly not familiar to him from any personal experience, but nevertheless reflected his newly-won state of mind, namely, concerning participation of a civil servant in political life.

> Guidelines for effecting Handbook of Administrative Practices regulations concerning suspension of duties (§§ 71ff. and 179)

> To all subsidiary departments:
> Consistent with § 71 and § 179 respectively of the law of 25 January 19. ., Gov't. Bull. Nr. 15 concerning the conditions of service of Civil Service Officers and State Employees (HAP), an Officer, Junior Officer, or Clerk in the Civil Service is to be placed in the Off-Duty Category:
> 1) if he becomes a candidate for the seat of delegate in a constitutionally sanctioned representative body (Reichsrat, Landtag) or is appointed to fill a vacated seat until the next regularly scheduled election, and
> 2) if he is elected as representative to Parliament and does not decline his election, for the duration of the regular term of office, or, in the case of appointment to fill a vacated seat, from the time he becomes a member of the representative body.
> A state employee elected to the Parliament is not to be placed in the Off-Duty Category. Where necessary, however, furlough from official duties in his depart-

ment should be granted during the exercise of his Parliamentary responsibilities.

Should an individual case, such as the election of a Civil Service Officer to a seat in a local representative body, require special dispensation beyond the authority of the department in question, then the case should be referred to the next higher authority.

Vienna, 4 February 19..
Suppl. 8745 Bull.44

A long, drawn-out row of columns fluttered by the bureaucrat's inner eye after reading such texts, like a sonorous musical scale. But that vision no longer astonished him; the direct relationship that had developed between his life and his book had become second nature to him (and that alone is the hallmark of a real reader as well as a real author). He paged on; and now the following emerged, as if from somewhere far back behind the row of columns:

Guidelines for effecting Handbook of Administrative Practices regulations concerning punishment for dereliction of duty (§§87 37ff. and 181 37ff.)

To the Directors of all State Financial Agencies:
1) The Law of 25 January 19.., Govt. Bull. Nr. 15 concerning the conditions of service of State Civil Service Officers and Government employees (HAP) includes, in §§89 and 181, the right of a superior to issue a reprimand to agencies under his jurisdiction and to point out to subordinates any improprieties in the execution of their duties, as well as authority of the governing body to seek compensation for costs / damages as expressly maintained and set forth in §§87 and 181 to the effect that Officers, Junior Officers, and Clerks who are guilty of offenses against the Service by virtue of disregard for regulations or failure to carry out their duties shall be subject to disciplinary proceedings.

2) The authority to impose punishment for breach of
regulations resides with the Disciplinary Commission
(§§113, para. 2, §§122, para. 2, and §§127, para. 2,
HAP, but additionally with the Chairman of the agency
in question as well as the Chairman of any superior
authority (§91 HAP).
3) In order to avoid any inequality in treatment of
Officers that might result from the above-mentioned
determination of jurisdiction in instances where a
monetary penalty may be imposed, the chairmen of
agencies and offices subordinate to the State Financial
Authority, in the event the imposition of a fine becomes a consideration, are to notify the State Financial
Authority of the initiation of disciplinary proceedings
and the surrounding circumstances. The imposition of
a fine can only be carried out 14 days after the filing of
such a report. The final dispensation in such proceedings remains within the jurisdiction of the State Financial Authority. Up to the point that dispensation is
made according to § 91, para. 3 HAP, the Presidium of
the State Finance Authority reserves the right to exercise jurisdiction over the initiation of disciplinary proceedings, their conduct, and the final dispensation.

The frightening character of the words and their tone, at first
like a stone wall rising up all around and beginning to arch overhead as if it wanted to close in and form a cavern of terror, was
eventually, when all was said and done, ameliorated by orderliness,
that reliable door that leads from the unfamiliar into everyday life
— once a person has found it, he knows he's been reunited with
his earthly home, where there's nothing incomparable, where
everything can be kept at bay and in perspective by comparison.
And therefore man endures ordered terror more easily and patiently, even though, basically, it may be much more frightful than
terror without order, which one is always compelled to confront
like someone who has stepped out of line — alone and confused.

Zihal read on:

(31) Cases submitted to the Disciplinary Commission are to be numbered separately (cardinal numbers) and entered in a dedicated record book. All items pertaining to an individual disciplinary action are to be displayed, numbered individually and consecutively, below the numerical heading assigned to the case when entered into the record book. At the conclusion of the proceedings, the records of all sessions are to be placed in an envelope of heavy paper on which is listed the Disciplinary Commission, the name of the accused, the service year in which the disciplinary action took place, and the number (cardinal number) corresponding to that under which the case was entered into the register. The envelope is then to be stored, in the same numerical order, in a locked cabinet.

Ground beneath the feet! Home ground! And in a flash, even Zihal's world resembled the polished faucets in the stairwell, the building in general, which looked like a modest, extremely neat, old woman, the grocer, Frau Zadichek, the mildness of the warmer seasons, the ponderous, hesitant sun of the late afternoon, for instance, out there in the local vineyards where they'd decided to go whenever the weather improved enough to permit it! And astonishingly enough, as if by magic, something related, something conciliatory jumped out of the book:

(32) In the preparation and submission of records of disciplinary proceedings for infraction of service rules or for personal misconduct, special attention should be given to the form in which items of evidence are presented, as far as this is compatible with establishing the veracity of testimony, so as to spare the accused embarrassment.

The bureaucrat lifted his head with a feeling of liberation, as if a constricting ring had fallen away from his breast. And in doing so, he looked over the roof of the building on the opposite side of the street and into a piece of fresh, warm, blue sky which was just beginning to free itself from the tattered blanket of clouds. A few moments later, as if it had been aimed, a sunbeam had already pierced the window and touched the open book like the point of a golden-yellow wedge which soon extended across the whole breadth of the room.

20

There was an explosion of beautiful weather, an assault — victorious on all sides. Just the way things used to happen in days gone by when a besieged city was stormed — if the enemy soldiers managed to get over the wall anywhere at all, the streets were soon swarming with them and their banners as they forced their way in from all sides — that was the way the existing damp and gloomy portrait of the sky simply crumbled to pieces and fell to earth everywhere; and just the way the rents and breaches in the wall of clouds were torn open more widely up there, so, here below around the sun-drenched squares, where one could see the dampness beginning to steal away from one minute to the next until its general retreat had become obvious, gardens flamed up bright green, and people gushed out everywhere — a hand of cards, showing only their gray backs up to that point, were now suddenly turned over and spread out on the table, revealing all their colorful figures. On the following day it was already warm, on the third, hot — something the spring always manages to accomplish quickly in Vienna.

The bureaucrat was dug up like a mole and pulled out into the daylight. In that sort of mood he was walking — as a part of the Stammtisch group, now distributed lengthwise along the narrow paths between the vineyards — next to Fräulein Rosl Oplatek, that is to say, in an already customary position that had been quietly approved of by all and sundry. Something intangible seemed to be weaving its way through the air, gently touching his face in passing; out of the question for it to be the drifting spider webs of fall — more likely the slanting beams of the inclining sun, now almost physical, like golden bars so dense that the view toward the opposing hills and down the valley into which they were descending was torn into diagonal stripes; and only now and then did the striking green from across the way flash through.

Past the little stone house in the valley — he wasn't at all amazed to still find on its windowless back wall, in monstrous black with gigantic yellow lettering — and with the picture of the heel of a shoe in the middle!— the same praise, just in larger format (not exactly an enhancement for the landscape!) as that which adorned countless shoe polish cans. The bureaucrat felt — without being in the least aware of how ridiculous it was — somewhat as if he himself had painted that advertisement there at just the right moment for it to be seen as they walked by, even by Fräulein Oplatek (who, understandably, disapproved of it as completely inappropriate for such a beautiful spot). The sun drove a golden yellow wedge into the valley which extended far into the distance. To the right flowed the brook. Fräulein Oplatek mentioned that Beethoven used to go walking there. Julius nodded seriously and now felt quite distinctly, deep within his own body, the presence of a fever; he could see it, figuratively, the way one sees a glowing coal in the belly of a stove; but it was not without its pleasant side — it warmed him in a sort of shivery-comfortable way. He was looking forward to the wine.

And beyond that he was looking forward to a part of the future, as yet unclear in its details, but certainly clear in its insistent approach and its need to be dealt with. But just now, for the first time, he was struck with astonishment, amazement at his walking along there, at the excursion in which he was participating — how had he been able to do it, manage to get himself there at all? And in the next moment, already feeling quite at home in the situation, he was aware of something like disdain, carelessness, and recklessness toward everything else and anything that had gone before. He offered Fräulein Oplatek his arm when there were steps along the way. She held on tightly to Julius. He suddenly believed he'd been dreaming for a few weeks, not really living; and simultaneously, now, (while the woman, Rosl, solid and round as she was, weighed against him a little heavily) he felt the two-layered basis of his existence lying crosswise within him, as if he could sense his own diaphragm; yet at the same time that life had awakened a heightened sensitivity within him, unlike anything previous, and a possibility of comparison so extraordinary that he had the absolutely physical sensation of stepping into another world.

The evening dissolved into a kaleidoscope of colors as they took their places at a simple wooden table in the rustic wine tavern: green fell away into gold and violet and in the sky above the Danube to the rear, the incipient sunset indulged in ever-increasing excesses, flared up in flesh-colored tones along its retreating edges and, in the center, sank into the smoky red of a bass fiddle. Next to the hurricane lamps the polished, frosted carafes of the new wine took their place, a gleaming, fluid treasure, lifted out of the depths of the cellar, still untouched and icy like a direct gift of nature and not the work of caring and confident hands — as if it had come pouring straight out of the vineyard without vintner, without harvest, without press. They hardly noticed the three musicians sitting to the rear in a slightly elevated arcade; the soft tuning of their instruments gave the impression of some natural sound from the deepening evening, but with the first swallow from the cold wineglasses, the music went sliding down their throats as well.

Considering Zihal's frame of mind, that moment would be only very remotely comparable to the one in the second part of Goethe's *Faust* where the homunculus is floating in the retort above the head of the venerable Doctor Wagner. But, indeed, the bureaucrat still found himself, as well, in a closed, transparent receptacle at that point, floating weightlessly, however, never bumping against the walls of the container, subjectively just as much outside of it as within it. At the same time, he knew he'd already experienced that condition or something approaching it or at least related, but it simply didn't occur to him that this had been the case just since a few days ago. Things had to take their own course here; as he was about to take Fräulein Rosl's hand underneath the table, she gave him a good squeeze and for a good, long moment, held his hand firmly against the curve of her hip. In addition, today she seemed — and immediately Zihal recalled a certain moment on the street, with the thin, racing moon in the sky — once again more relaxed, reclining on her broad hips, as if on Juno's throne of clouds. The music wove its decoration of golden ribbons around the table and those who were sitting there laughing and talking.

A jet of soda water was propelled from a siphon bottle with totally unexpected force by the pressure of excess carbonation and shot between two of the people sitting at the table, who leaped aside, screeching. Doctor Döblinger could be heard saying, "There appears to have been a djinn sitting in the bottle." "Gin is what you call the English juniper schnapps," noted Zihal, "I drank it in Paris myself as a young man." "No, this is a different djinn," yelled Dr. Döblinger, laughing, "this is an evil spirit from an oriental fairy tale, not the juniper spirit at all — he was kept prisoner in a bottle the same way, but he escaped and got into mischief." Zihal's hand was resting lightly on the broad cloud bank in which Dame Juno was sitting beside him; the touch carried him for a moment to the dizzying height of the Eiffel Tower. Only then did it happen, in addition, that she pressed her hand, warm and full, on his. "Can anything of the sort ever have happened?" inquired the bureaucrat of Dr. Döblinger, but at that instant he was preoccupied by a completely different image: that very day, before riding out to the agreed-upon meeting point, the bureaucrat had once again looked in on the cabinet maker whom he'd commissioned to make the table needed for the observatory. It now seemed to him — because he'd been in somewhat of a hurry — that he hadn't exercised sufficient care in emphasizing to the craftsman the need to stay within certain measurements; and besides, those measurements had only been conveyed in terms of an estimate (as a first approximation). Here, now, with his inner eye on the problem, it seemed suddenly to be a matter of complete indifference to him, separated from him, behind a partition almost, an intervening wall; well, earlier on he'd certainly never worried about finishing or not finishing up with some file or other while he was drinking wine! (He managed a second's self-reproach). In fact, the thought soon collapsed impotently. Zihal took a mouthful from his glass and glanced at Fräulein Rosl, whose face looked somewhat serious, a little flushed, perhaps even tender, but at the very least quite pretty. The wine was taking effect. "Can anything of the sort ever have happened," said the bureaucrat, turned toward Dr. Döblinger, repeating his earlier question and using his words to erect a folding screen or window blind over there.

"Strictly speaking, things like that have always happened and it's no different today," said Herr von Döblinger, laughing, "and, furthermore, nowadays one no longer has to be so completely convinced that there even are so-called 'dead' things. Everything's living, just a little bit different in tempo, flies faster than humans and rocks the slowest of all. But, all joking aside, isn't there really something like a demonic side to objects? No? There really are completely ordinary scissors with which you've cut yourself so often that it finally dawns on you, or cooking pots that creep over to the edge of the counter again and again — just those and not the others — in order to try to fall off, right? ('Oh, yes!' called out two ladies at the table) Such things are animated by ill will, possessed by a spirit, a 'djinn' like the one in the story of the Thousand and One Nights."

"Herr Doctor," said the bureaucrat, who was now showing a sudden interest here, which was perhaps deep and lively enough to cause him to smile sardonically in order to cover or obscure it, "you know that I hold you in great esteem (now the whole table fell silent and listened — Herr von Döblinger as well, with an unusual attentiveness that had something malicious about it), you know that . . . by all means, I grant you that in advance. But you also are aware that I, for my part, never read novels; I've always been a serious person, my whole life long, a widower too, and never read novels for the very reason that, for the most part, such things just excite a person unnecessarily in a certain sense. We understand each other. (Rosl now looked at him very attentively, but respectfully as well. The silence of the rest of the group seemed to cast him and her together, to press them against each other in a benevolent way — the fluidly palpable way in which they all shared his feelings lent the bureaucrat, as it were, a loftier base, behind which the rolling waves of his now so distant and yet

ever-present pain were quieted.) My profession demanded seriousness. So you'll probably be amazed when I tell you now that I'm
quite taken with the business about the demon in things and am
listening with interest, genuine interest. I can confirm what you've
said. (He took a drink from his glass at this point; he found himself
in a holiday mood there, to a certain extent, on vacation and on
safe ground; in his own tavern he would never have dared to think
or say such things, which, in the end, despite seriousness and an
enlightened attitude just came down to certain demons, demonesses, and djinns in bottles.) I'm just simply a human being, like we
all are. And every one has his weaknesses. I've had to learn that,
too, Herr Doctor, and often a person really doesn't know where
reason stops and superstition begins. Or whether reason hasn't
vacated the premises long ago and is living at another address,
namely, with superstition. There can even be such a thing as a
reasonable superstition. Please. I'm not laughing at anyone. Man
is in general quite alone, quite alone (he'd quite gradually and
dimly become aware that he'd slipped his arm beneath Rosl's
while talking; she'd permitted it and so they went on sitting in that
way.) Well, that's the way it is, Herr Doctor. Was wonderful, what
you just said then. So, cheers, everyone!" He smiled again. It was
probably a trifle sardonic — not in any way meant for Fräulein
Oplatek, but directed, instead, at himself, because he had to
concede something in effect, admit something: for example, that
they were all just human and they all had their weaknesses or their
bottles, genies, demons or demonesses. The wine was taking effect.
At any rate, the bureaucrat's speech seemed quite impressive to the
entire table — they all cheered him, stood up and clinked glasses
with him and Rosl. To be precise, the way it happened was that one
by one they made their glasses ring against the pair of theirs.
Doctor Döblinger ordered more to drink.

It was Rosl who now settled them down again, finding her more
resolute tone, strict and upright and newly constructed from the
various firm blocks of her personage: "If you're always this nicely
behaved, Herr Councillor, one could easily turn a blind eye toward
the weaknesses of mankind and all that. But, I have to tell you, the

word is 'take care' because people are watching you — oh yes, my dear man, just so you know: everything's known, we know it all. We even know your housekeeper Frau Zadichek — well, no wonder, for ten years she's been doing her shopping there, in the little market near us . . . "

"You live there in the neighborhood, too?" asked Julius, who at the mention of his Zadichek's name had given a gruff, but good-natured grunt; but at the same time a dividing partition shoved its way through him again, his gaze deepened and darkened, it took on a degree of similarity to a certain glinting, nocturnally dark, double-eyed apparatus. For several seconds he sat there like only half a man, simultaneously really a little shocked by Fräulein Oplatek's words for about as long as it takes to draw a breath. "Where do . . . ?" he started to ask. Two different mechanisms were working within him, separated by his diaphragm. "So just remember, Herr Councillor," said Rosl, after she'd named the street where she lived, "just remember that I'm always near you. And it's a known fact that women notice everything." "That's occasionally true for men as well," replied Zihal and watched that bold statement disappear the way one follows a perfectly round, blue ring that's been produced totally by chance while smoking, knowing full well that it couldn't be done purposely. Right afterward, he once again felt his approaching pain, and amazement, amazement at everything, especially at this way of living that was completely new to him. It was as if his mouth was filling itself with a new language that wanted to displace the one he'd previously spoken. The immediate result was that he fell silent; there was a sort of hardness in his mouth, as if his oral cavity had been lined with stone for the last several moments. He drank and it soon went away.

On the way home, he walked behind with Rosl on the way down into the valley to the streetcar terminus. The Stammtisch had again reformed itself into a line along the path next to the brook. Their arms were entwined, their hands as well, and they walked slowly, then gradually even more slowly. In the darkness in front of the bureaucrat, memory had hollowed out a space for itself, was hovering ahead of him, moving away from him as if it were falling back further and further to avoid his steps, but enveloping him, to the right and left of his face, with fine threads that were being pulled along like a net, with him in it. Was perhaps a new sack of the most delicate material being mysteriously woven around him here? He wished it were so for those few moments, in fact, wished it very much. It would be the end of everything, a sudden arrival after a strangely circuitous journey. In that space of memory in front of him he saw the dark doorway through which he had walked into his equally dark, back room once upon a time, when his earthly sky full of stars had calmly and mysteriously presented itself to him and become visible in its silent splendor. Beautiful is what it was, to stand there in the dark and look so deeply within and so far out beyond. And now the lights of the city below and in front of him moved him quite surprisingly as they stepped around a fork in the way and around a thicket where the warm air of the day had collected. He turned toward her, the woman standing beside him, who'd softened in the darkness, a cloud, a junoesque cloud, waiting there, without movement. The most startling thing happened: the last layer of air between them gave way, then he'd embraced her and kissed her on the mouth, and she held her mouth out to him again, and what he'd previously seen only with genteel, sidelong glances, he now felt in the darkness — close, powerful, meant for him, just him. Of one thought, they immediately hurried off to catch up with the others and were able to unobtrusively take their places again in the long, drawn-out Stammtisch group a good distance before reaching the streetcar terminus — pretty, round Rosl and the bureaucrat who by then was about half-grown.

21

Herr Wänzrich failed to appear: once, twice, then permanently.

On the second evening, during a brief check from Window III, the bureaucrat discovered that the blinds were lowered and closed at "view downward and to the right."

The bureaucrat's upper lip, with its little moustache, puckered sourly and full of disgust; in the moonlight that had now become fainter, his head looked almost like that of a rabbit. What this meant was obvious: treason. But, although there was the new and intensified risk of a — disgraceful — counter-observation, Zihal remained by the window without taking any particular precautions and studied the dark panes opposite him more intensively; from there, the enemy had once demolished him with coldly aimed fire and caused him to sink.

On the following day, Zihal was unexpectedly confronted by Herr Wänzrich, who immediately came dancing and prancing across the vestibule, offering repeated obsequious greetings. The bureaucrat, stepping back with dignity to avoid being touched by one of the innumerable tentacles, surveyed the party who had failed to keep his appointments and said curtly, but nevertheless with good humor of the official type, "Well, young man, we don't get to see you at all anymore."

"Not at all anymore, Herr Councillor, quite right, not at all," said Herr Wänzrich, who let his lewd eyes roam all over Zihal and then, still smiling, more closely studied the bureaucrat's jacket and hat, collar and tie with invisible but palpable impudence. "Not at all anymore, quite right, but of course I remain humbly grateful, even though all of those pleasures are, of course, over, finished — but still, eternally grateful. In the meantime things have progressed to the point of personal acquaintance, I have arrived there, have made my way to the pure maiden Margit, the very same, Herr Councillor, with whom I am in love, have persisted, have made my way. Have spoken with Margit — among other things of my honorable intentions — who, considering the pangs of my love, my exalted wishes if I may say so, offers sufficient nourishment through frequent proximity and provides the encouragement for me to strive onward in my aforementioned honorable intentions. Therefore, pleasures of the previous sort, of the sort of enjoyment now behind me, if I may say so, will be left behind, all of those observations, I mean observations of the pure maid in particular, all observations of that sort. Allow me to wish the Herr Councillor — who has looked upon my youth with so much sympathy, such kind understanding — continued great pleasure, enjoyment of a degree consistent with such things, that is my wish for the Herr Councillor. I, myself, leaving all that behind me will remain, henceforth, cleansed of it; the Herr Councillor will doubtless approve of that, comprehend, understand. The personal element prevents such things henceforth, strictly the personal element, the element of love which I feel, in other words, in the trust and purity which we enjoy to the fullest at this point, in other words, briefly stated, the personal element, Herr Councillor."

"The personal element," repeated the bureaucrat very slowly; "Of course, in your case a renewal of your permit would be necessary as well, but, considering the circumstances, there is little likelihood that one would be granted, even if you were to make application. Well, best left as it is." He touched the brim of his hat fleetingly with his index finger as a hint, then simply left Wänzrich standing there smiling and bowing repeatedly and began to climb the stairs with his upper lip furled to its fullest and his moustache twitching.

His anger knew no bounds. He had no intention of going out again that day; a fragile, feverish feeling in his bones and joints again warned him that he should at least stretch out on the sofa for a little while. But then, in the general attack that was finally beginning — unleashed by his disgust for that faithless dilettante, who was pitifully chained to a single, wretched object — in that attack that whistled as if it had been compressed through a narrow pipe, all traces of tiredness or exhaustion had evaporated. The important thing was to find a way to resist his own, depressing anger, to find the quickest way to outrun the powerless disgust, which that miserable situation was constantly and ever more violently eliciting from the bureaucrat. Within him it was rising like icy swamp water; outside, it was running down him like congealed batter.

He kept his hat on his head. However, he felt no sense of haste, just the opposite — each movement was carried out with gravity as if he were trying to wall himself off against the emotions he'd suffered and which were burning within him. His chin and mouth felt like they were made of stone. From a small, iron lock-box

Zihal took the entire amount he'd withdrawn from his savings account, which corresponded to the price of the already selected telescope, inclusive of the estimated cost of the observatory table. The sunlight in his rooms, the silence in which they remained far behind him, so to speak, as he got ready to leave, all of that penetrated him — and for just a brief moment he felt weak again — like a deep-seated, yet indistinct pain in the vicinity of the diaphragm, a slow dissolution or displacement of one's self into one's concealed, unknown organs. He put the money into his pocket carefully.

For the first time, out in the warmth of the streets, beneath the tent of blue sky that had been put up and which now and again flapped in the faint, balmy puffs of wind, he was carrying through the city — openly and by light of day — a most definitive plan from a different and darker floor (beneath the diaphragm). He was no longer creeping around in troglodytic caves at home or just feeling around outside and exploring only with catalogues; now, on the good citizens' sidewalk, life was headed down properly organized, official channels.

The closest agency at hand there functioned with improbable speed and ease. Scarcely an hour after he'd left home, Zihal was already rolling up to his door in a "one-spanner"— back then there were still such one-horse cabriolets in Vienna — loaded down with heavy artillery. It was expertly packed and the bureaucrat was not only in possession of, but well acquainted with, the instructions for its use. Naturally, the optician would have been happy to have one of his employees deliver the instrument to the bureaucrat's home, but Zihal, shaking his head mutely, insisted on immediately taking it along with him in the carriage.

Carrying it — expertly packed along with its tripod — under his arm, he came around the first bend of the staircase and caught sight of something going on slowly and with a lot of maneuvering: two workmen were carrying a heavy table made of unfinished, four-square, planed boards (which actually didn't look too big) up through the stairwell. Something clicked in Zihal, the way switches do beneath a fast train as it coasts into the station and the feeling was just the same as it had been in the past, back at the beginning of that strange journey when he'd discovered for the first time the possibility of terrestrial astronomy and had projected the coordinate system of tax-office orderliness onto a new universe, almost as if he were being squeezed by the claws of the eagle with two heads which had just plunged down out of the ether-blue heaven where concepts dwell. Then, however, Julius had been alone, concealed, like a moth that had burrowed deep into a fur in a closet; later, one evening, there had been two of them — or, actually, at night, at night. Now three of them — during the day, of an afternoon, in the afternoon in other words; he was outside in the stairwell, passing the doors of the other apartments, accompanying this transport column of two cabinetmaker's helpers (or was the one just an apprentice?) because he couldn't get past it at first, the stairway was too narrow. He managed to do it quickly at the next landing and as he did, shamefacedly introduced himself to the two men with the table. Julius flew on ahead as quickly as was consistent with carrying the telescope carefully. Behind him the transport column heaved and pushed. There was a lot going on there in the stairwell, things had spread out, become substantial, even crude compared to what we started with — that delicate little moth in the closet. It seemed to the bureaucrat as if he were leading, almost publicly, a whole troop, a procession, a retinue. Those two cabinetmaker's helpers: that was just too much, it was more than too much — as the French say, "c'était de trop."

Enough of this being charmed by our Julius's strange solo number, his frenzied carryings-on in a lonely moth's burrow. Real life now stepped in, lent form to things, a good deal of form — with its awesome goodness and indulgence — at the least, right then, in the form of the sweating workmen behind Zihal and the expensive, heavy tube in his arms; the latter had to be put down carefully somewhere, doors opened, there had to be some yelling back and forth, the table had to be carried through and into the back room — through an apartment split open by so much reality: on two, three, or even more tracks, things were humming along beside the moth's solitary burrow. Polyphony instead of a single voice. Indeed, everyone is eventually returned to the maternal breast of life, no matter how divorced from it his carryings-on might seem; and every flagship of painful, total orderliness will eventually sink like the Flying Dutchman, finally redeemed. How many are rotting away at the bottom of the sea, turning into organic substance piece by piece, bit by bit!

He was left alone. The sun persisted in skewering his two rooms on an angle, then gradually burned down like a candle and turned red. Order still held sway there, bristling in the silence, causing martyrdom all around, demanding the most painstaking unwrapping of the tubular package (alien, but appropriate to the task as it lay on the bright, new table, it suggested the path of an explosion that had split the apartment in two), the folding and putting aside of the large amount of heavy and lighter wrapping paper, the careful rolling of the string into little balls to be saved, the cautious opening of the special box in which there was more paper, fine paper, tissue paper, like tissue, and finally the removal of the tube itself from its case . . . the edges of all those pieces of paper stared, rustled, stuck up in the air, cut the room into pieces.

There had scarcely ever been such a moment of tension in that life, not even on the wedding trip to Paris, not by a long shot. And not only that, but by light of day, actually during the afternoon, the late afternoon, already getting along toward evening, so, then — in the evening. One could now proceed with arranging the table properly so as to set up the telescope, put it in position for a test. Zihal felt surrounded by a dry heat, but with his attention focused so closely, he really only noticed it when he suddenly felt a severe chill and a little bit of dizziness that made him put his hand on the edge of the new table for support. And that new table seemed to be a lot smaller than Julius thought it was going to be! There were always problems with tradesmen, as soon as one got mixed up with them at all; he clearly should have given the measurements more exactly, not just in terms of an estimate (as a first approximation). "It feels like I have a little bit of fever . . . humph, certainly no wonder at all, considering what's going on at the moment," is what he thought, literally. But things would work out anyway, despite the apparent smallness of the table. "Nevertheless it can be considered satisfactory and steps can now be taken to proceed with mounting the telescope on its tripod according to instructions." It was absolutely beautiful: the legs extending and snapping into place and the unspeakably smooth, frictionless swivelling in every direction. Outside everything tilted, liquefied, and evaporated in the nearly absolute silence as the sun began to set, blue with gold; and in the opposite direction, the almost cup-like, empty blueness had decorated itself with all sorts of curlicues that drifted off and swam in the distance. The evening sun settled against the buildings like a casually directed word which made their faces light up.

However, the little sack that had shrunk and was at that point surrounding the bureaucrat even more — but still securely tied shut — allowed the sensory data from the external world to pass through only like a factual report: that it was getting on toward evening, for instance, or that the sunset was beginning to glow. The sack acted like a filter that allowed only abstractions to pass, as it were, but didn't allow a more or less fluid transition from inside to outside, which is really the actual, human condition, since one basically doesn't know exactly where one's own person ends and the external world begins; at most, one knows it in a physical sense. Zihal's situation, however, included a boundary drawn with unusual sharpness, life based purely on his own inner reserves, which immediately and violently resisted any attempt at restocking from the outside — an orbit in a closed planetary system, a sphere separated by invisible walls from any and all communication.

One in which a technical question presented itself for resolution: whether it would be better to set up the telescope directly on top of the table with its tripod legs extended all the way like a daddy longlegs', or, on the other hand, collapsed into a stumpy-legged thing that would likely be more stable and then set on the — even if ominous or odious — smoking table after the latter had been lifted onto the planed surface of the table, the accoutrements on top of it having been previously removed and stored respectively, in line with a decision reached earlier. The somewhat terrifying daddy longlegs was picked for the first trial, then a chair lifted onto the observation platform, onto which the bureaucrat climbed with the help of a second chair. Space was at a premium. The feet at the ends of the bug's legs were not very far from the edge of the table at two points. Zihal, now seated, had to extend his own legs in between them with care, avoiding sideways movement at all costs.

Next he decided to immediately carry out a preliminary observation and put the instrument to use for the first time according to the printed instructions, aiming randomly at some distant point in the neighborhood. He bent down, his brow against the eyepiece. With considerable diffidence he turned the focusing adjustment, and then suddenly, at the slightest twist of his hand — after disappointment, indeed, even fright had tried to interrupt — out of the watery, totally indistinct ripples that had filled the tube thus far leaped the decorated cornice of a distant building, torn loose by the hand of a colossus and hurled toward him, gigantic, gray against the background of the sky — landing directly in front of the mouth of the tube, three feet away, with never-appreciated details, cracks, and fissures.

The bureaucrat practiced the procedure several times. He learned how to use his instrument. Extended and black, it protruded from his forehead into the surrounding quiet of the evening, a body part that he'd produced, a horn of fate. With irresistible force it sucked the bureaucrat into itself and, with a whirling motion, hurled him out into the distance; simultaneously, Zihal realized that this was the first time he'd looked out into such distances while it was still light. It was probably because of the tube, whose mighty extension could no longer be concealed under cover of night — it protruded, it stuck out into the softly veiling dusk like a piling out of water. It was a bridge that joined two worlds, and axis about which they now both rotated.

As he swivelled the tube, everything blurred immediately, leaped away from right to left in a rapid flood of gray, watery ripples into which the setting sun poured the red of spilled tomato sauce. Zihal soon realized that, with such a powerful instrument, letting his searching gaze simply wander around was something that could only be accomplished by very fine, gradual adjustments; since everything appeared so large and near at hand and two or three windows of a distant building were enough to fill the entire field of vision, rapid swivelling would make it seem as if Zihal were running or flying along the fronts of one or two houses in half a second, in which case, naturally, he couldn't see a thing. Under such a constraint his hands became more precise within a minute, capable of carefully adjusting the scope. Sitting there, the way he was now, behind the spider-tripod, our Julius looked much more like a scholar — an old-time *Astronomus*, for instance — than an admiral doing battle.

Because — and the following remark cannot easily be suppressed at this point — the more sharply one sees things, the more it becomes necessary to move through life in general with careful and delicate adjustments, while the half-blind calves just go galloping all over the place. Whoever sees quite sharply, hardly even moves at all any more, indeed, some people diligently avoid any movement, just in order to be able to see. However, they represent an element whose behavior already exceeds the bounds of the permissible and against whom official action has not been taken simply because the aforementioned individuals know how to keep themselves beyond the focus of official eyes by virtue of their lack of motion.

Now, of course, Julius had to learn that the positions of stars can't be determined in the daylight, a finding also valid to a certain extent for terrestrial astronomy — particularly in the case of very tiny, distant stars and especially when one proceeds directly to the use of a very powerful telescope, which presents to the eye an abundance of previously unappreciated, but now quite prominent individual details. Take the matter of perceived distance: many things are pushed apart that previously seemed to be located right next to each other (just as they do to the naked eye when looking at the sky at night!), and when an individual object then appears totally isolated within the field of vision, often all sense of orientation is lost. It seemed advisable to the bureaucrat to leave his observatory sighted in, at least in a crude, general sense, before it became completely dark; he climbed down from the table, having for safety's sake made the final decision to use the scope with short, fat legs set on top of the little smoking table and as he went about arranging things that way, he was suddenly struck by an ingenious idea for simplifying orientation in the terrestrial starry sky: namely to use the Sixty-Sixer as the transition between the naked eye and the effect of the telescope which so altered the world out there. As a result things were set up — as a marginal comment — just the way they are in every observatory: next to the large refracting telescope there are several small tubes, the so-called "comet spotters." Hoisting up the little smoking table was carried out without difficulty and, in fact, it was more comfortable for Julius to sit behind the eyepiece that way. As he now set the Sixty-Sixer down under the tripod (next to the registry, tablet, pencil, and lamp), he was overcome by a strange feeling of calmness, of relief, so that he snuggled down into that transient sensation for several moments, while simultaneously, isolated images from the excursion out to the vineyards in the country rose and fell before his mind's eye: a blast of soda water shot from the siphon bottle, Doctor Döblinger talked (and he chuckled at that point) about the spirit in the bottle, whose name sounded like the English juniper schnapps he'd once had in Paris. He picked up the Sixty-Sixer again and tried to look at it jokingly or soothingly, as if they both were in agreement (and during such meditations that had arrived and slipped in unnoticed — but as irresistibly as the dusk — the bureaucrat remained totally absorbed and motionless). But the lenses of the field glasses gleamed — cold, dark, and deep. The daylight began to wane. The telescope, slanted, long, stiff, and obstinate as an old fashioned collar, stood out against the failing light, black on gray. Since everything was set up and well-prepared, Zihal got ready to go out (without turning on the lights in the already darkened apartment, of course), carefully locked up, walked down the empty, silent stairs on his way to get something to eat. Within him, ravenous hunger battled against lack of appetite, each claiming victory in turn, over and over again.

22

Everything felt different. Every blood vessel was bursting with resolution. Nor, in the face of the prevailing and crystallizing reality, was Zihal lacking in a certain heroic element, in the sense of those famous words, "I have dared." (However, the reader may rest assured that neither Latin nor a ringing tone is going to come up here — that experiment has already met with resounding failure.) The fact that almost achieved, tangibly close perfection makes a person shudder because of the coldness of that which is exemplary (of the museum-like, one could say)— that's something Julius had to learn too: perfection simply separates itself from life, indeed, actually before it has been realized and tangibly reached, before one has laid a hand on it. If the last stretch of the road leading up to it appears to the human eye (and indeed the bureaucrat had already become something akin to a human being) to be accessible, open, and able to be traversed with certainty, then everything — namely, the entire, exciting stretch of the road that has been traversed up till then — already seems to have been rendered barren, devoid of sense, and incomprehensible, scarcely even worth recalling. To explain it another way: while he was walking along the street, whatever his back room now held in terms of highly perfected preparations existed in Zihal only in what might be called a geometrical way, with the pure lines of geometry or like a crystallographic model (erotica more geometrico). The sensation had become threatening during the afternoon, with wet, smooth, deeply hollowed-out troughs between waves. Now it stood there as dry as the parched lips of someone with a fever, as tense as a vein below a tourniquet. He just couldn't warm up to it anymore.

He avoided his usual restaurant. He avoided everything in general, every contribution which the outside world might perhaps be inclined to make to his current situation, the faces of people on the street, even the face of a friend who said hello . . . everything that came toward him or tried to enter was hostile, had to be hostile, because it could obscure the short, straight, leveled prospect at which Zihal was staring. He wanted to walk on securely at all costs. At that point, of course, he felt as if he'd been tied up and handed over to capricious chance without having exposed himself to it ("If everything just works out all right"— that's what life depended on now!) and he looked out of the corners of his eyes, full of hate, at every projection, every streak of light, every movement which the world around him thrust into his path. And so, carefully withdrawn into himself like a clam or hermit crab, he was finally sitting over his meal in a tavern he'd never been in before, opposite a paneled wall painted bright yellow, where newspapers, clamped in their wooden holders, hung from the coat hooks. It remains, despite Zihal's somewhat unhinged condition, completely understandable that he would have wanted to take down a newspaper; and of course, here it's clear that one does not generally do that in order to learn something new (unless there've been unusual events or unusually troubled times). Zihal had no interest in the news at that point, quite the opposite — a sort of embargo was actually in force within him. But the point was to make a familiar motion, one with which he might be able to feel his way through a bit of the time that lay before him, separating him from his goal, exposing him to the hostile whims of chance. He surrendered to the automatism of the reading eye, which informed him about things that had nothing to do with him at all; however, he was dependably numbed by the general character of the public news, sterilized by the smell of newsprint and ink, swimming in it much the way the corpses in the Anatomical Institute swim in their formaldehyde. In such a state, no one is obliged to bother about his previous life. A newspaper is the best screen against real life and by reading it, you become more and more like your overcoat hanging on the hook; indeed, you've already hung yourself up next to it, a garment without a body — through its lifeless shell the thin little spirits of the news dance like swarms of mosquitoes.

But Zihal did not take a newspaper down from the hook. The movement of getting up would have been too much for him, indeed, would have appeared to be a bold extravagance, a challenge to walk a tightrope at the most unfavorable moment. Beyond that, he suddenly realized with horror — with horror because it seemed an ill omen to him — that he'd left his home for no good reason at all, because he had absolutely no appetite, not in the least. So what was he doing there then?! He thought quickly and quietly to himself, mousy-gray, so to speak, in the soft shadows of consciousness of the fact that, after all, one could even be run over out on the street. When the meal came, he had it again — his appetite, that is — but after a few bites it disappeared just as quickly. Zihal ordered some wine, took a big gulp of it just as the door from the bar was pushed open, depositing a load of noise in the room, unloading it with a clatter, smashing everything to smithereens. "Hey, neighbor!" yelled someone who walked over toward Zihal from behind, and then, because the bureaucrat re-mained quiet as a mouse, tottered back out again in the expansive way that drunks have. It became quiet, the door banged closed, the side room where Julius was sitting was empty as before. Perhaps the waiter had restored order again.

The bureaucrat got himself out of there in a hurry. He slipped out into the darkness of the street like a mouse running into its hole. What was awaiting him just a short time hence burned dryly within him, just as his lips did beneath his moustache; they seemed to have small, tender spots. He meandered through various streets, always staying close to his own neighborhood, all the while feeling uncertain among the numerous people who were walking around there, rushing by, turning in somewhere, either into a building or a shop — just the things happen on the street if the evening hasn't progressed too far. He no doubt saw all of that, but saw it in a way that kept it at a distance, as if he were looking at the world through opera glasses turned backwards — it was distant. However, even at that distance it preserved its legitimacy, in the honking of an automobile, the ringing of a streetcar's bell; its institutions carried on, the path of duty continued on its course. It was just that Zihal had to reject it at that moment, couldn't use it, wasn't ready just then, wasn't open for office hours, had postponed all of his appointments. He very definitely felt that the situation was one of great weakness, of being exposed. In fact, for several moments he was quite consciously (he had indeed become almost human) surprised at where he'd actually ended up; and then he escaped from the street into a café that was totally foreign to him.

There a newspaper was lying on a table. Soon Zihal was hanging beside his own coat and the news was running out of his sleeves again. Even the steadfastness of time was unable to resist being inundated that way; it soon dissolved, crumbled into big pieces the way a sugar cube does in water, and in the end — as if awakening from the faint buzzing and aching that accompanied his own somewhat elevated body temperature — the bureaucrat found that he needed to get a move on. Indeed, he was swirled away by the rapids in relative disorder — he stuck his change purse into his overcoat pocket rather than, as he always did, into his left pants pocket, and then outside on the street was frightened out of all proportion to the cause when he felt in the usual place and failed to find it. A similar thing happened later with his house keys — and here his heart skipped a couple of beats as deep, accusing anxiety tried to insinuate itself throughout the entire moment; he kept missing his house keys almost obstinately, even though they were in their usual place in his right-hand pants pocket, just because his shaky hand didn't reach deeply enough into the corner. One could say that Zihal started up the steps with reins hanging, then even stumbled noisily. At the same time he could feel the sweat on his skin, like a damp cover that had suddenly been thrown over him.

Meanwhile, the great moment itself, when he would take his position behind the new telescope, approached completely dryly, a little stiffly, a little geometrically, one might say; and in the darkness, the cool and alien feel of the powerful instrument made itself known to his carefully probing fingers. Beside Zihal, so to speak, already independent and perceived by him as an external fact, stood the incessant trembling of his hands — which disturbed him about the way a fly would — and, soon, of his limbs and his whole body. He didn't get very upset about it though — only to the extent of thinking that his stupid excitement was going to ruin everything! He accepted it, filed it properly, charged it up, as it were, with the other details of the current situation, and thus managed, despite all, to operate his optical instrument precisely.

All of that had nothing to do with the fact that the bureaucrat, immediately after he entered the darkened room, had set into motion with his firm grip an unforeseen but powerful series of events, in the sense that the decision he suddenly fired off into the dark and its execution came together precisely at one point: walking up to Window III, in his hand the Sixty-Sixer which he'd picked up securely, but with a flourish, from its temporary position beneath the tripod, he sent a stern, parallel-chambered gaze over to certain blind, dark-as-night windows, one of which was clearly standing open again. The bureaucrat disdained examining it more closely. For a moment, things became as white and cold for Zihal as the moonlight that would have split open the room at such an hour not long ago; and now, just in his memory, he seemed to glow with an icy whiteness for several moments, just as he did then. "View downward and to the right" was permitting a soft, warm light to filter through the lowered blinds and out into the darkness. The bureaucrat opened the inner section of his window and found a cord wound around a button; the device which he'd never used before now obeyed him without a hitch, and with that self-contained and presumptuous exclusivity with which, for example, someone stupid will interrupt a shy person who's speaking, the roller blind came clattering down and blocked the view. The straightforward obedience of the mechanism gave Zihal the feeling that his impulsive action had been appropriate and correct.

But now he was already seated on the bridge, our terrestrial-astronomical admiral, and giving orders to the stars: Window II, opposite! He'd long since learned his old star chart by heart — outmoded would be more accurate, because the new telescope would even create new relationships in space, project a new system of coordinates onto it, displace the zero-point. At the relatively short distance from "II, opposite, 10 o'clock," it was now only necessary for the previously utilized comet spotter to determine if an object had already appeared there. Yes, that was the case; it appeared — large, black-haired, and with a sudsy gleam — in the literal meaning of the word, namely, using hot water from a bucket. Zihal deftly swivelled the tube, whose lack of resistance and adjustability at any angle alone were sufficient to give deep satisfaction. Immediately things glowed in front of his eye like flowing, rippling fire; with an extreme effort to control the trembling of his hand, Julius carefully altered the focus of the eyepiece and now, suddenly, that curtain of wobbly gelatin dissolved and into the room across the entire breadth of his field of vision plunged a glistening, soapy shoulder and even more — the white-enameled bathtub in which those strapping legs were standing; and simultaneously, to the rear, many details of the furnishing of that distant room, which now seemed to border directly on Zihal's observatory, separated from it only by a glass wall. The bureaucrat jerked his head back, knitted his brows, and hunched his shoulders, then twisted a little to the side — in short, he took cover. The girl had just about looked him straight in the eye.

What a first look into the depths of terrestrial space! Eye to eye with the unfathomable — enough to make anyone dizzy! Julius got a grip on himself with considerable effort by thrusting his unassailable situation and dominating position into the foreground of his consciousness (indeed, he didn't just know how to read his book and use his instrument, but had just recently begun to develop, as well, the ability to make skilled adjustments on his own internal cogwheels!). And so he now surveyed, beaming and in total composure, the breadth of neighboring space. It was a triumphal, enchanted entry into worlds of experience that several months ago had still lain deep within the shadowy nucleus of the never-suspected, the nonexistent. But (and how tiny, puny, and insignificant Herr Wänzrich appeared now, scrabbling like a bug far beneath the bureaucrat) . . . but, no matter how urgently individual details might force themselves on him, no matter how large the lumps and bumps which the world of the senses now presented to him — indeed released on him with all the formlessness of an avalanche — the law of the totality of objects, operating from deep within the bureaucrat, held its ground, even if shakily, even if all of its extremities were trembling. It was a matter of storming a new heaven, not being diverted by an individual star! (Even if he constantly seemed to see, out of the corner of his eye, a twinkle from a tiny greenish-blue star which hadn't even risen yet!). Zihal directed the telescope out toward more distant objects; and with the gentle, careful swivelling of the tube (which gave him such intense pleasure), the countless increasing, growing, then over-growing components were subjugated in advance by form — a system was born in which the locations of those new stars could all take their places. Now, for the first time he really understood his instrument and loved it, since it had given him the inspiration for a new cosmos of orderliness, one that was infinitely expandable. Every angle of inclination or change of direction could be read off, in fact, from a small half circle marked with gradations which was fastened to the base on which the telescope swivelled (for this purpose, of course, the flashlight had to be modified for use that close to the window by letting the batteries run down at bit and adding a suitably constructed paper hood). But the primitive method of designating the various observation settings ("view downward and to the right" or "directly opposite"), while sufficient for a scarcely developed star world, now became a thing of the past; and the same was true for the childish, fairy-tale names. Forest Nymph was now called, for instance, II 136°/22°, 10 o'clock. No, better still, no words at all (like "o'clock"), just numbers and even the symbol for degrees could be dropped: II 136 22 10. And as far as the intensity of illumination was concerned, as well as the ranking of the object with regard to impressiveness — for the latter, a scale using standard Arabic numbers would be acceptable and at the same time could function as the reference number under which the object would be displayed in the complete registry. Then the intensity of illumination could be appended, using small letters to indicate rank. Accordingly, it would look something like: 126) II 98 15 10:30, f. (One can see that the bureaucrat hoped — not without justification — for a high yield.) It was a new age with a new language. Additionally, whatever lay at the level of zero degrees elevation or below would be recognizable as optically favorable by the number alone. For elevation of the telescope, however, an upper limit would have to be established; cases located still higher would no longer receive an index number and would be excluded from the list. Practically speaking, however, such a regulation would hardly ever or at most, rarely, be applied, because the observer's position itself was a relatively elevated one; in addition, the part of the city that spread out in front of Window II was located on a slight incline. Only one further prerequisite for this new method of data entry needed consideration (Zihal had already made preliminary plans to put it into effect the following evening), namely, that a precise designation of the observation settings would only be possible if the positions of the observatory table as well as that of the little smoking table and the three tripod legs on top of it remained constant — which could easily be accomplished by means of precise (scratched) marks on the floor as well as on the observatory and instrument tables, respectively.

These conceptions went gliding by unopposed, indeed to the exclusion of everything else, on a swift current within Zihal — he had become immediately and totally immersed in that flowing and swirling of ideas, where one segment joined another one and pulled it along, rushing off in great haste. Thus all the threads were rearranged in his once again recreated world, just as soon as the basic facts of its existence offered a central point toward which they could all be drawn — the zero point in a new system of spatial coordinates. That swirling sequence of images and conclusions which all hung together loosely, as if they'd been attached to one another with an office ring-binder, had incredible power (to which, as a matter of fact, reading a newspaper could hardly be compared) and, all things considered, a certain depth as well, even if the loosely attached material presented there might not exactly give that impression; be that as it may, much that was quite distant, things that lay quite far back temporally, came to the surface of consciousness thereby (like dead deep-sea fish, churned up by volcanic activity at the bottom of the ocean, now floating on the waves). For instance, traversing more than twenty-five years with the graceful steps of a ballerina — practical scientific material from the time of the "pressure cooker" course and the "Intelligence Test"; and it was no surprise that it was immediately put to use: degrees, angles, and how to locate a point in space.

His head had drooped somewhat, to the right side of the eyepiece, as if he were staring into another, deep tube in which all of those things were swarming around — that's how much the principal of order was being swamped at that moment by a literally blinding mass of material, theory, practice, form, content. Well, he was superior to certain people, the bureaucrat, far superior; he considered himself in a position of superiority. Even his shaking had disappeared. However, when he straightened up once more, it immediately returned. At the same time, a disturbing feeling crept over him, as if, perhaps, he were hollow inside or sitting on air. Zihal held his breath, got up slowly and carefully and felt down along the legs of his chair; one of them was now located quite close to the edge of the table, indeed, still on it by only a centimeter's breadth. "The sizes are mismatched," he thought, "have to keep that in mind." With that his problems were banished for the time being and he took his seat again.

That he did with his inner orientation completely in the direction of the Forest Nymph — she still carried her old-fashioned fairy-tale name, but that nonsense was soon to be abolished and she herself torn from the sky and brought directly before the bureaucrat's eye — and the same for all the stars! Besides, anyone who would list their positions according to numbers no longer believes in nymphs and fairies. Here was lost, as well — in that new wave of the general attack — the memory of his deep-seated, pious respect and knightly bearing toward the Forest Nymph. But there was no going back. The transport column had labored all the way up the stairs, the horn of fate had grown far out of his forehead, staring out into a world of objects that had been torn away from their remoteness and demystified. In the face of the instrument, all things were the same. Could he now relinquish that power — even though conferred by the external world — as well, the single viable nerve that was left to him, the only one he possessed at that moment? He would have fallen into emptiness, died quietly of thirst in senseless isolation, from which no other springs bubbled.

Nonetheless, he really did fall into emptiness now, if not inwardly, at least outwardly, with his eye — instead of the reddish constellation of the Forest Nymph there was mute, uniform darkness. The star had not risen, even though long overdue — perhaps completely burned out. It would be better to assume that the Forest Nymph had fled from the rising new age to a different space — beyond, with reference to Zihal's cosmos that is, otherworldly compared to the latter, and yet, not entirely.

She was sitting at the home of her friend, the Countess Langingen, in a room in which the predominant violets and whites collided in a not particularly tasteful way. The curtains had been let down and one could not see into the park, but anyway, it was dark outside. The little Venus in the glass case above the women didn't like the evenings simply because one could not look out and drift with the clouds on the shimmering river of memories in which everything flowed as if it had been cast in delicate porcelain; and she liked it least of all when there were visitors at the palace, because the conversations that went on, compared to those she'd once heard long ago, seemed quite silly. Today, however, several sentences struck deep into the unmodeled layers within her where the past was loyally preserved — several sentences which the Forest Nymph below (her reddish dress was a splendid example of barbarism, there in that room) was reading to the Dowager Countess from a book bound in blue, whose color also collided horribly and incessantly with the violet all around, the whole setting illuminated by a long-stemmed lamp with an "abatjour."

"Isn't he charming?" exclaimed the Forest Nymph and went on reading: "There is nothing more profound, more mysterious, richer, more veiled, more glowing than a window illuminated by candles. Nothing that is observed in broad daylight is as captivating as that which takes place behind a window pane.

"Above the waves of the rooftops I caught sight of a woman ripe in years. She has wrinkles already, is poor, is always standing bent over something, never goes out. From her face, from her clothing, from her movements, almost from nothing, I have reconstructed the history of that woman, or, better yet, her legend, and I tell it to myself sometimes, weeping."

The Forest Nymph went on reading for a long time. When she had concluded, up fluttered those breathless and fragmentary figures of speech with which cultured people indicate their delight with art. The naked body of the little Venus in the vitrine, however, glowed through the soft light as if some greater tension were animating her faultless skin of porcelain, as if deep inside there were some upheaval in the pure substance from which she'd been made, because she had recognized those lines by her long-dead friend, the poet whose room she'd shared — she'd been there when he wrote them down and had even heard him reading aloud what he'd written. Now his fame had outlived him, had even made its way through to those two ridiculous women, who, left to their own devices, certainly would never have discovered a poet . . . As always, she thought of his eyes this time, too, dark as tunnels leading into his head and simultaneously she was delighted to be able to sail away from those ladies on the cloud-ship of her memories — even though she was deprived of the view into the park with its trees and the little, stone pavilion — and into the slowly changing sky. Now a little whirlpool arose, dark, as if India ink had been cast into it, the few decades following the death of the poet were easily lost within it; over time, however, things that belonged together ended up side by side. And in that category belonged the big, deep eyes of that old gentleman who had been there, at the battle of Königgrätz, and had lived next to her at the way station for migratory souls; and who, it seemed to her, was just as little inclined or capable of relinquishing his own soul there as she herself would have been. And she suddenly realized how beautiful it was to become old, very old, ancient. Where might he be today, that good, old Excellency? Certainly not there. Refined people pass through distressing times as if through transient exile.

One star dies out, a new one begins to glow. "What's going on out there in the cosmos?" a person asks himself, for instance our learned Astronomus behind his telescope. However, it's obvious:

nothing's happening that doesn't somehow concern the person who's asking the question at that moment, doesn't have some connection or other with him.

Julius Zihal may have sensed that dimly. He gazed at the lifeless, black hole that had developed out there as if he were looking into a dead place within his own self, an incomprehensible one: there was the defect in his system, so to speak, the significant breach in the restraining ring of total order. Amidst the blaring trumpets of the general attack, the flute-like voices of other possibilities wafted in from out there, transiently known even to him from spiderweb-gentle caresses that were totally resistant to categorization in the assured world of objects.

He now fled from that so eloquent darkness, after a quick glance off to the right which indicated that the tiny, greenish-blue star, which reminded him of its existence over and over again by a sparkle in the corner of his eye, inhabited only his mind for the time being, having not yet risen above the distant horizon — but, of course, it was still too early. Comet-spotter in hand, he cast himself, with a momentarily completely cool, totally resolved motion (more geometrico, as it were, with which he now had to fill in the gap that had developed within him) out into the remote distance. Already using his instrument more skillfully, he became witness to a totally unbelievable scene in a corner or tower room, where a scrawny and slovenly looking older woman was painting a door with white enamel, brushing away dedicatedly, and apparently satisfied with her work too, because she'd just cocked her head back to observe it. At that very moment a tall, fat man opened the freshly painted door, walked into the room, and, without further ado, gave her such a violent slap in the face that she dropped the paint pot and fell back, fighting for balance. Completely unmoved, the bureaucrat redirected the telescope. No matter how much people carried on, no matter how urgent they made it sound, whatever did not fall within one's own area of jurisdiction was turned away with ears of iron, at best accompanied by the mention of a room number where presumably such cases would be dealt with. Indeed, even here as well, he was implacable toward nonsense and stupidity that was out of place and toward disturbances of that sort in his field of vision in general.

However the scope simply gathered it all up and, with tremendous power, pulled in everything that presented itself; and so, totally unexpected blows could be dealt by the eyepiece, coming, so to speak, from the pressure of the light beams suddenly shooting in from interstellar space; then, of course, the air would be displaced with such extreme force that for entire moments the observatory chair would almost float, and everything would be so violently shaken that it wobbled and trembled.

In that way, like two meteorites, the two beautiful sisters or friends from far out beyond suddenly flew directly at Zihal's head as they gracefully crossed the threshold between their room and the bathroom that lay behind it, frequently stopping beside one another, arm in arm. For a whole, long moment It seemed to our Julius as if he and his chair had become quite tiny and were hovering in front of the eyepiece, ready to crawl into it. His trembling could no longer be controlled and in his excitement he edged a little closer with his chair, then remembered the relative narrowness of the observatory table and settled down. The searing gleam of that constellation "Bilitis" was soon extinguished; however, still preserved within it was the light from the open bathroom door, whose rectangle was framed by the now darkened front room; then it was closed, but as that happened, an excerpt from the previously enjoyed images revealed itself in a flash of light, like a persisting vision.

At that very moment the tiny star "Green-Blue" appeared above the horizon to the right.

The comet-spotter in Zihal's hand trembled so inordinately that he could scarcely get it up to his eyes. The first thing he was able to establish — and it ran through all of his limbs like a stimulating electric current — was that his estimation of the altitude of "Greenish-blue" was exactly correct. He was located on the same horizontal level as the constellation, perhaps even slightly above. Two windows were clearly illuminated and free of curtains. The moving nucleus displayed a sky-blue color today, likely from a blouse or jacket, or a sweater, a knitted sweater.

He swivelled the telescope as if he were sitting isolated high in space, in empty, totally enveloping, finely sparkling ether. Again the tube filled itself with distant, streaming fire that stood there in a sort of gelatinous brilliance, as if a jellyfish were being trans-illuminated. As it tore apart, Zihal, knees trembling, dived directly at the lighted windows like a night insect. Behind them, someone was emerging from the blue sweater; and more rapidly than the bureaucrat's powers of comprehension were even able to follow it all, consecutive stories of a personage were already being erected over there out of firm, blossomy-white blocks. Now he completely lost control of his extremities — they moved constantly, fluttering spasmodically, and in fact he was still holding on to the thought that this was all due to the poorly judged dimensions of the observatory table, but he couldn't hold on to it tightly enough and finally let it drop in desperation, now driven by the sole impulse to crawl completely into telescope behind his own bulging eyeballs. Just as, at the beginning of an anesthetic, one may still feel this or that, distantly, as if from rooms in the soul which one has vacated, so he perceived out there, at the border with the rest of life — which he'd allowed to go on its own way — a certain hollowness, a sitting on air, which, however, didn't bother him a bit in his hunched-together, bent-over position; and that reassuring thought was simultaneously the last, vaguely perceptible statement from his sense of balance.

Into that closely applied, vapor layer of the tangibly close fulfillment of his dream, however, there suddenly poked a trilling, incessant, and increasingly loud ringing of the doorbell — outside, someone must have forcefully and purposefully pressed his thumb against the button.

23

It pulled him out of the tube into which he was trying to crawl the way a corkscrew extracts the cork from a bottle. He had to straighten up to the sound of the continuous, wild ringing: now something was demanding attention that hadn't concerned him at all previously — and then fright skewered his body from top to bottom as the left rear leg of the chair slipped from the edge of the table into the void, causing a sudden, wild spasm like a belly-shaking hiccough.

What followed was an unavoidable fall, to which Zihal simply resigned himself — a good thing, because that way he was more relaxed and didn't fall hard enough to break anything. The telescope went too — his hand reached up for something to grab on to and knocked it off balance. And beyond that, the little smoking table was lifted up as the bureaucrat's feet shot up from beneath it, said little table adding itself to the tail end of the avalanche and causing — after Zihal's groaning fall and the heavy thunder of the telescope falling on the floor — an ugly, disreputable, bleating noise of a lighter caliber.

Well — what do you say now? What was he to be "considered as" now, our bureaucrat? Is that what he still was? No, that's no longer a bureaucrat; whatever's thumping and bumping around there amidst the darkness and destruction can hardly be designated as such any longer. It is . . . chaos.

The absolute nadir; and at that point, there's no such thing as rank, no revisors, no councillors.

For several seconds our Julius plunged down, deep into primordial chaos, as if he still wanted to have one last go at finally becoming humanized; and so Zihal remained motionless amidst the wreckage, one broken piece among the others in the darkness.

Then he rose up, uninjured, to his full stature and took the first step as a new person — to the light switch.

And there was light. For the first time, the harsh gleam of an electric light bulb leaped into the remotest corners of his troglodytic cave and provided an illuminated finale to the battlefield of Julius Zihal's late-life evolution. The latter straightened his clothes and tie with dignity. The light was turned on even in the front room. He walked through it and, as he did, gave the inward appearance of a tidied-up, freshly whitewashed room, hospital-clean, virgin-pure. As he approached the entrance door through the kitchen, soft steps hurried away from it — interrupting the previous motionless listening — then down the steps in a hopping, almost melodious way, then ran away, distanced themselves, took themselves off into the distance. Zihal got the whole picture. He opened the door nevertheless, with complete composure, but saw no one. Then he went back into his rooms. The fever he'd been suppressing for a long time now shook him quite unmistakably. To the last chords of the totality of order, he set about cleaning up the scene of the disaster. Slivers of glass trickled out of the telescope as if it were a half-empty bag. Zihal gave no impression of being upset, merely one of sadness. He went for the dustpan and brush. Calmly and resignedly the remains of the scope, the tablet, the registry, and the lamp were stowed away in the lowest drawer of the dresser, which was then locked. He put the key in the adjacent desk. Zihal even took out the stored smoking accoutrements again and lined them up on the little table which had remained un-damaged, still feverish but getting used to the shivers and the fact that his hands couldn't entirely be trusted. Everything was done slowly and at a constant pace, something like the way people walk in a funeral procession. The chair was missing a leg. He carried the pieces into the kitchen. Then he pushed the big, new table back into its usual position in front of the window. During all this elaborate going-on, Zihal mumbled three words to himself from time to time: "The personal element. The personal element."

Now, for the first time, he picked up the Sixty-Sixer, the only thing which had remained undisturbed and in one piece on top of the observatory table, because Zihal had put it down there — not on top of the little smoking table between the stumpy legs of the tripod, but curiously enough, under his chair. Quite amazed, he picked up the blackish instrument from the bright, planed surface. He checked the lenses and focusing screw and then sighted, quite cursorily, at a distant light — the glasses were still in working order. Zihal put them in their case with its blue silk lining and then openly hung them by their strap over the nearest clothes-hook.

That having been done, Zihal's strength drained away so rapidly that his legs, shaking from fever, were hardly able to support him any longer. He was still able — and these last chores were carried out in a state of near unconsciousness — to close the window, take off his clothes, find his way to the bed in the dark, and get in. There, finally, with his teeth chattering, yet with a luxurious feeling, he crept deeply into his own fever as if under a glowing blanket, toward the flickering light that seemed to be pouring forth in front of him like some hot, purifying bath of absolution for anything and everything, a purgatory.

24

The genie had finally gotten out of the bottle. This is what appeared to be the background cause of all the frightful things that subsequently occurred and it was this which first provided the terrifying setting for those events: the unfolding to giant size, like a hatching dragon, of the Double Eagle after it emerged from the Sixty-Sixer. Now everything became clear, because it was sitting in the background of the Great Hall of the Parliament and had reached out with its talons to take over the proceedings. From there came its thunderous voice.

And Zihal, humiliated and burdened more than usual, filled with heavy, oppressive worry because of the two cabinet-maker's assistants, was frantically trying to get to his appointment without being able to move from the spot. There was no doubt that today the trip to the parliament building was going to take two or three times as long as it did under — now gone for ever, of course — normal circumstances. Because there in the suburb, his way was blocked everywhere by extremely dangerous, horny claws attached to the ends of long tentacles or polypoid arms which were emerging from cellarways all over the place, like wine-delivery hoses that had come alive and were now writhing in the gutters here and there in bunches, feeling the sidewalk with slow, silent, coiling movements, causing the horny ends to clatter — one of them struck out hard against the heel of Zihal's shoe as he hastened away.

At the Ringstrasse, the most humiliating path that Julius had ever had to tread appeared to be unequivocally blocked.

From the side, coming out of the red fortress, a column of

demonstrators was moving toward the House of Representatives, occupying the whole width of the Ringstrasse, similar to 1910, when the workers marched on parliament demanding universal suffrage — everything red this time as well, in strings and endless chains, looking from a distance like red worms creeping along and wriggling around each other.

Seen up close, however, the worms were columns of huge bugs walking on their hind legs in rows of four. Marshals accompanied the procession at intervals on the left and right. Those organizers, especially fat and red, were tied to one another by a long, glittering chain which consisted of countless small paper clips hooked together. In that way they kept everyone headed in the same direction and, at the same time, cordoned off the line of march from the dense masses of spectators on both sides, in one of which Zihal, oppressed by rage and desperation, had been forced to come to a halt. Now their chants could be heard:

> *"Because of illness, due to sickness, on account of illness*
> *due to unbecoming illnesses, unbecoming*
> *because of sickness, due to illness,*

> *"Because of excess, due to excess, on account of excess,*
> *due to unbecoming excesses, excessive*
> *because unbecoming, due to excess,*

> *"Because of the personal element, due to the personal element,*
> *on account of the personal nature*
> *due to unbecoming elements, due to personality*
> *because of personality, due to that element."*

"Pigs!" growled Zihal, embittered in the extreme; but they weren't pigs, they were just bugs. And faster than he would have liked it, he was suddenly pushed through the crowd — indeed with considerable pressure — as if he were being batted up the ramp of the Parliament building by fists and right into the interior. An extreme fear over the finality of his entrance took hold of him, while long rows of columns fluttered past his gaze. Already his whole mouth felt like stone, like a petrified cavity of terror which merely expanded and took on the form of the mighty Hall of Delegates, whose background was completely occupied by that figure so feared: squatting gigantically, with its folded wings jutting toward the ceiling like mountain peaks, bathed in a gold that was misty-bright from anger. Enraged and impatient, it scraped its talons, while up above, flaming tongues shot out of the twin heads. Julius pressed himself against a white marble column where he ceased to exist, became totally flat, like a painting, or really, more like a spot, a disgusting one, on the stone. And yet, what was spoken now by the thunderous voice echoed within him as if in the endlessly deep spiral vaults of a conch shell:

> "Civil Servants who are afflicted by an illness, other than those designated in §62. para. 1, by virtue of their own misconduct (Article 5 of the Pension Regulations of 26 March 1781 in the revised version of §2 of the Law of 14 May, 1896, Gov't. Bull. Nr. 74) are to be considered as having become ill in a fashion inimical to their profession and unconditionally forfeit any claim to continued pension benefits if said benefits have already been drawn for more than a month and if the personal element appears in an incriminatory light."

It penetrated deeply into his belly, ice-cold. In a mysterious way, it meant something much worse than just the loss of one's pension.

"You may go," someone said coldly and loudly from off to the side.

Zihal heard himself screaming in desperation and that scream spanned a bridge from his dream into wakefulness and was so reverberating and evil in the darkness of his room that, for several moments, Julius lay there in his own goose bumps as if they were chain mail. Only then did the darkness fade somewhat, warmed again and obscured by the flames of fever behind his eyelids.

25

On the following morning, Frau Zadichek could tell at a glance
that the bureaucrat was sick. His bedding was changed, he was
tucked back in snugly and given only herbal tea and toast for
breakfast. Frau Zadichek paid about as much attention to the new
table by the window as she would have to a child's toy that had
been left in a corner somewhere. In the course of the day, Zihal
was checked on no fewer than seven times by his housekeeper, to
see if he needed anything and to bring a nourishing oatmeal soup
at noon. In the evening just before nine, she came up to visit him
once more.

He felt well, incredibly well. It was a feeling of health that had
seemingly descended on him from above, an aura that covered
him. He rose, dreaming, into the empty sky above the late-life
battlefield of his existence the way the moon sometimes does
above real battlefields, where, with the very edge of its light it
absentmindedly even fluffs up the earth a little, then smoothes it
out, its hand gnawed at by jagged things — the gable of a house
whose roof has collapsed, the hulk of an overturned tank, the rigid,
upright knee of a dead man. Unmoved, the moonlight weaves on.
Unmoved, the former bureaucrat floated above everything that had
been, maintaining the same distance from it everywhere. And so he
merely smiled when it occurred to him only after the fact that Herr
Wänzrich had no doubt seen him working on the telescope late that
afternoon, standing out and easily visible in the sunlight that
flooded the room. And probably that was the way he'd gotten the
idea for his nocturnal foray. And that was all right — it was meant
to be that way.

The sun returned again in the afternoon, and Zihal fell asleep as
its reddish beams touched the barred shadows on the wall like
ghostly fingers plucking at mute strings.

On the morning of the following day — with Zihal in a much
improved state and feeling reborn, bathed, and, at the same time,
cultishly hungry — anyway, on the following morning, without
wasting any words, Frau Zadichek brought the shaving things to
the astonished Zihal's bedside; he obediently — if somewhat

cowed — put them to use, while she adroitly held the mirror, obviously resolved not to leave him until his appearance had been restored to a proper degree of dignity. She even brought the wash-basin filled with warm water and carefully washed off his face. Following that he received a clean nightshirt, his moustache was straightened up, put into the trainer and his hair combed. "Herr Councillor is going to have a visitor this afternoon," she said significantly, to the accompaniment of an alto undertone which moved Zihal strangely — and then left him before he had a chance to ask her anything more.

But beyond that, she came back at noontime as well, as he was taking off his moustache trainer, and while he was eating his oatmeal soup, satisfied his curiosity with nothing more than a meaningful smile and the words "Herr Councillor will soon find out." She seemed preoccupied with whatever was going on. Her gaze assessed the orderliness of the room; again she made no mention at all of the big, new table, but did take the moustache trainer from the night-table and hang it, not, as usual, from the nail that had been driven into the headboard of the bed, but next to the other excrescences along the edge of the oilcloth cover on the wash-stand. Then she hurried out.

Julius hadn't heard the bell ring (Frau Zadichek must therefore have been waiting right at the door); but no doubt he'd already recognized that a guest, someone about to visit the sickroom, had come in, just from the careful and hesitant way the door was opened, even if no one had knocked previously.

Directly behind Fräulein Oplatek came Frau Zadichek wearing the beaming and delighted expression of a magician who's just managed to pull a pigeon out of his apparently empty top hat.

Rosl, planted firmly and maternally on the collective, well-ordered stories and firm blocks of her personage said, "And how is the Herr Councillor today?" and in the same breath begged his pardon for forcing herself on him; but Frau Zadichek had told her about the Herr Councillor's illness and she just had to allow herself to see how he was doing. "Well, apparently getting better already?" she added with a glance at his soigné appearance, which she may well not have expected.

His confusion and heartfelt emotion did not remain hidden from her; he held her hand for a long time, and squeezed it. Just to say somehing (because what she was thinking was that our former bureaucrat looked so dear and nice lying there in his little bed — "Great staging, Frau Zadichek!" is what you feel like yelling from the audience!)— just to say something, she went on about the Royal Opera, which she was going to attend that night for the first time in her life. Two complimentary tickets had been made available to her by the Postal and Telegraph Administration, and she had kept one of them — a parquet seat at that! Of course she had a nice, dark dress — so far so good; but what she didn't have, unfortunately, was a pair of opera glasses and she had her doubts about the hygiene of the glasses they rent. It was the same reason why she never borrowed books from the library.

Julius asked what was being performed that evening.

"The *Magic Flute* by Mozart," she said. They both fell silent. On the wall the bright sun began its silent play on the strings of the shadow-harp. "Here are some glasses," said Zihal and Frau Zadichek handed over the Sixty-Sixer. Immediately afterward she felt that the moment had come for her to disappear, with a smile which revealed the benevolence of the higher, suprapersonal charge, which she had now fulfilled. "Rosl," said the bureaucrat. She bent down to him. And after they had embraced, he added — in a tone that made it clear that his words were quite serious — "Keep the glasses, as a favor to me and in memory of this day." She nodded mutely.

And with that our story is over. All that remains to be pointed out is that all those related events conspired, on that memorable day, to finally bring a certain old Excellency who'd been present at the battle of Königgrätz into the Imperial Opera House, which recognized him just as little as it did the Postmistress Rosl Oplatek, because it had only been built after the time of our Sixty-Sixer. The little Venus at Countess Langingen's had been quite right in her view that refined people pass through distressing times as if through transient exile.